Simeon Pease Meads

Chemical primer : an elementary work for use in high schools, academies, and medical colleges

Simeon Pease Meads

Chemical primer : an elementary work for use in high schools, academies, and medical colleges

ISBN/EAN: 9783337156763

Printed in Europe, USA, Canada, Australia, Japan

Cover: Foto ©Paul-Georg Meister /pixelio.de

More available books at **www.hansebooks.com**

CHEMICAL PRIMER:

AN ELEMENTARY WORK

FOR USE IN

HIGH SCHOOLS, ACADEMIES, AND MEDICAL COLLEGES.

BY

S. P. MEADS.

→THIRD EDITION.←

W. B. HARDY,
GENERAL AGENT,
961 BROADWAY,
OAKLAND, CAL.
1884.

ENTERED ACCORDING TO ACT OF CONGRESS IN THE YEAR 1884,
BY S. P. MEADS,
IN THE OFFICE OF THE LIBRARIAN OF CONGRESS, AT WASHINGTON, D. C.

PACIFIC PRESS,
Printers, Electrotypers, & Binders,
OAKLAND, CAL.

Preface to Second Edition.

THIS Primer has been prepared for use especially in those schools that can give to chemistry only one term's work. It has grown out of the needs of the class-room, as I have felt them. Its statements are necessarily somewhat narrow, confining the pupil to general rules. Refined accuracy means a treatise, not a primer. I have given in the following pages as much as I think the average class can digest in a single term, and I hope my fellow-teachers will carefully examine the plan *throughout* before passing judgment.

I have freely consulted whatever chemical works were within my reach, especially Attfield, Barker, Roscoe and Schorlemmer, Eliot and Storer, Appleton, and Jones.

For criticisms and valuable suggestions in preparing this Second Edition, I am indebted to Prof. Joseph LeConte and Prof. W. B. Rising, of the University of California. I wish to acknowledge my obligation to many teachers who are using my humble work in their classes, especially to Prof. Geo. R. Kleeberger, of the State Normal School, San Jose, and to Mr. Volney Rattan, of the Girls' High School, San Francisco. Nor should I forget my indebtedness to Mr. C. B. Bradley in the preparation of my First Edition.

An experience of three years in teaching chemistry to medical students has enabled me, I hope, to anticipate their wants in several directions. It has shown me how greatly they need an elementary book before opening the excellent but voluminous works which should be their life companions.

Natural Science Dept., S. P. MEADS.
Oakland High School, Jan. 2, 1884.

Preface to Third Edition.

THE unexpected exhaustion of the Second Edition of this work in the space of six months, for use in the schools of California alone, has made it necessary for me, in order to meet the demand, to send this Third Edition hastily to the press. I have taken the opportunity to make a few needed corrections in the plates, and to put the book into a more attractive dress. I wish to express my hearty thanks to my fellow-teachers for their kindly appreciation of my efforts to present plainly and *tangibly* to beginners, the A, B, C, of chemistry.

Oakland, California, S. P. MEADS.
Aug. 1, 1884.

BRIEF SUGGESTIONS—MIXED.

DO not allow pupils lazily to pronounce the symbol or the formula instead of the name, *i. e.*, wherever "H" occurs, see that it is called hydrogen..... Have the pupils copy the two Reference Tables (pp. 16, 29) upon cardboard, and allow them the free use of these for the entire term. Never compel them to memorize formulas, atomic weights, strength, etc. It is as important to know what not to remember, as to know what should be remembered, since the former comprises by far the larger portion of any text-book ..... Let the pupils perform all experiments (except, perhaps, a few difficult ones, or for the sake of taking your turn with the class) in presence of the class, explaining each experiment as it proceeds. It takes time, but it is the only way to teach chemistry where a table for each student cannot be provided. If you haven't time, omit half the experiments to accomplish this result. Assign to separate pupils one experiment each a few days beforehand. The experiments may be performed upon a plank table (see FRONTISPIECE), costing not over four dollars...... *Every* experiment teaches something, and the sooner you can impress this fact the better. While you should make every experiment as impressive as it can be made, get the pupils through the babyhood which craves noisy or showy experiments, as early in the term as possible.. .... See that a number of larger works upon chemistry are at your desk for reference...... After you have passed the "Reactions," encourage any pupils *who may show a special liking for the science* to work out after school hours a number of solutions (not too complex, and mixed by you) by the Analytical Charts. ...... Teach pupils to use *small flasks* (test-tubes answer well) and *small quantities of chemicals*. It isn't necessary to burn a forest to prove that hydrocarbons are combustible, nor to blow up a continent to prove a substance explosive...... Don't be afraid to teach anything contrary to the text, *if you have good authority for it;* but let disputed points alone. Teach any simple principles beyond the text, instead of others more complex omitted; but don't teach intricate matter outside of text, else the result will be pupils will know neither the text nor the "intricate matter."...... Remember that one of the chief ends of a small text book in science is to teach the pupil to read intelligently larger works. .... Spend at least half the time in reaching carbon, page 63. ... .. Use the METRIC SYSTEM throughout; it is *the* system...... Use either thermometer. The CENTIGRADE (C) is used in this book, though the corresponding Fahrenheit (F) degrees are given in a few places.

INDEX.

	PAGE.
ACID, ACETIC	121, 132
" Benzoic	133
" Boracic	85
" Carbolic	121, 137
" Carbonic	66, 159
" Citric	124
" Gallic	124
" Hydrochloric	75
" Lactic	160
" Malic	124
" Muriatic	75
" Nitric	59, 60
" Oleic	16, 130
" Oxalic	124
" Palmitic	16
" Picric	147
" Prussic	58, 78
" Salts	140
" Stearic	16, 130
" Sulphuric	81
" Tannic	124, 125
" Tartaric	124
Acids	25, 135
Aconite	127, 136, 158
Air	34, 47, 58, 67
Albumen	122, 134, 156
Alcohol	119, 120
Alkalies	25, 136
Alkaloids	125, 127, 136, 157
Alloys	91, 143
Alum	148, 154
Aluminum	105, 106, 154
Amalgam	91
Amber	133

	PAGE.
Ammonium	61, 62, 114
Ammonia	60, 61, 62
" Type	125, 126
Anæsthetic	59, 120, 121
Analytical Charts	162, 163
Aniline	126, 147
Antidotes	133
Antimony	91, 152
Antiseptic	81, 97, 111, 112, 121
Aqua-fortis	60
Aqua-regia	60, 75, 152
Arsenicum	88, 135, 152
Atomic Theory	10, etc.
Atmosphere	34, 47, 58, 67
Atoms	10-13, etc.
Atropia	127, 158
BALSAMS	133
Barium	109, 155
Bases	25, 136
Basic Salts	141
Beer	119
Belladonna	127, 158
Benzol	70, 121
Bessemer's Process	102
Binary Compounds	11, 17
Bismuth	104
Bleaching	74, 81
" Powder	74
Blowpipe	53, 71, 94, 162
Borax	85
Boron	85
Brass	143
Bread-making	122

INDEX.

Brimstone ..... See Sulphur.
Bromine 76
Bronze 143
Bunsen's Burner 70
CALCIUM. 107
   " Light 108, 154
Calomel 97
Camphor 133
Candles 69, 130
Caoutchouc 133
Carat. 93
Caramel 117
Carbon 63
Carbon Dioxide 66, 159
Carmine. 143
Cast-iron 101
Cellulose 116
Chalk 108, 135
Charcoal 63
Chemistry of Candle 69
   "   " Cooking 122
   "   " Cleaning 131
Chlorine 72, 150
Chloroform 120
Chloral 121
   " Hydrate 121
Choke-damp 68
Chromium 92
Cinnabar 96
Clay 87, 106
Coal Gas 70
Cobalt 104
Cochineal 148
Coin 143
Coke 63, 70
Collodion 116
Compound Ethers 120
   " Radical 18
Combustion 34, 48, 49
Copper 100, 134, 154

Corrosive Sublimate 97
Cotton 116
Cream of Tartar 124
Creosote 121
Crystallization 56, 145, 146
Cupellation 95
Cyanogen 78
DAVY'S SAFETY LAMP 71
Deliquesence 56
Dextrin 116
Dextrose 117
Dialysis 158
Diamond 63
Diastase 118
Diffusion of Gases 52, 58
Disinfectant 50, 64, 73, 121
Distillation 57, 119, 120
Dyeing 147
EFFLORESENCE 56
Elements 16
Essences 120, 132
Etchings 60, 77
Ether 120
Ethyl Hydrate 119
   " Oxide 120
FATS 128
Fermentation 118, 130
Fireworks 111, 155
Flame 69
Fluorine 77
Formula, Empirical 115
   " Rational 115
Fusil Oil 120
Fusible Metal 104
GALENA 98
Galvanized Iron 103
Gas, Illuminating 70
Gelatin 122, 125
German Silver 143

INDEX.

Glass	86, 87
Glue	122
Gluten	122
Glycerin	130
Gold	92, 153
Graphite	63
Gum Arabic	116
Gum Resin	133
Gun Cotton	116
Gunpowder	111
Gutta-percha	133
Gypsum	108
HALOGENS	27, 72
Hard Solder	143
" Water	54
Hematite	23, 101
Hydrocarbons	48
Hydrogen	50, 149
Hydrogen Sulphide	82, 162
INDIA-RUBBER	133
Indigo	147
Ink	73, 125, 132
" Printers'	73
Iodine	76
Iron	101
Isomerism	115
LAKE	148
Laudanum	127, 136
Laughing-gas	59
Lead	98, 103
Leather	125
Lime	107
Lime-light	154
Linen	116
Litmus	25
Litharge	65
Logwood	148
Lunar Caustic	95
Lye	129, 136

MADDER	148
Magnesium	34, 106
Malt	119
Manganese	105
Marble	108
Marsh-gas	70
Matches	83
Mercury	96, 153
Metals	92
Methyl Alcohol	120
Metric System	160
Milk	122, 134
Miscellaneous Questions, 45, 78, 138	
Molasses	117
Mordant	148
Morphine	127, 136, 157
Mortar	108
NAPTHA	110, 112
Nascent State	63
Nickel	104
Nicotine	127
Nitre	111
Nitrous Oxide	59
Nitrogen	57
Nomenclature	17, 24
OILS	128
Olein	128
Opium	127, 136, 157
Organic Acids	124
" Bases	127, 157
" Chemistry	114
Oxides	34
Oxygen	46, 149
Ozone	50
PAPER	116
Paregoric	127
Pearlash	111
Pencils	63
Petrifaction	86
Pewter	143

8 INDEX.

	PAGE.
Phosphoresence	84
Phosphorus	83, 137, 151, 152
Photography	95, 96, 153
Plants, Office of	67
Plaster of Paris	108
Platinum	94, 149
Plumbago	63
Porcelain	87
Potash	110
Potassium	110
Quartz	86, 93
Quicksilver	96
Quinine	127, 157
Reactions	33
Reference Table I	16
" Table II	29
" Table II.—(con.)	160
Resin	133
Rochelle Salt	141
Rosin	133
Sago	116
Sal-ammoniac	60, 114
Saleratus	111
Salt, Common	112
Salts	25
Salts, acid, etc	140
Salts, Epsom	106, 135
Salts, Glauber's	113
Salts, Rochelle	141
Saltpetre	111
Sand	86
Selen-salts	142
Shellac	133, 155, 158
Shot	143
Silicon	85
Silver	94, 153
Soap	128, 131
Sodium	112
Solder	143

	PAGE.
Solution	37
Spectrum Analysis	143, 144
Stalactites	108
Starch	115, 122
Stearin	128
Steel	102
Strontium	109
Strychnine	127, 136, 157
Sublimation	80
Subnitrate of Bismuth	142
Sugar, Cane	116
" Grape	117, 155
" of Lead	99
Sulphur	79
Sulph-Salts	142
Tapioca	116
Tar	70
Tartar Emetic	91, 124
Tin	103
Turpentine	133
Type-metal	143
Verdigris	100
Vermilion	96
Ventilation	68
Vinegar	121, 136
Vitriol, Blue	100
" Green	102
" Oil of	81
Volatile Oils	132
Water	13, 14, 37, 53, 139
" of Crystallization	55
" type	26, 125
White-lead	99
Wines	119
Woody Fiber	116
Yeast	118, 123
Zinc	103

CHAPTER I.

INTRODUCTION.

MATTER exists in three states:—

1. **Solid:** Ex., iron, lead, ice.
2. **Liquid:** Ex., mercury, bromine, water.
3. **Gaseous:** Ex., hydrogen, air, steam.

Nearly all substances ordinarily in the solid state may, by applying *heat* (and removing pressure), be made first liquid and then gaseous. Nearly all gases, by *cold* and *pressure*, may be made first liquid and then solid.

A change which *merely* converts a solid to a liquid, or a liquid to a gas, or *vice versa*, however wonderful such change may be, is not a chemical, but a physical change. Ex., Ice may be heated and converted into water, a liquid, and then into steam, a gas.

All such changes are studied in *Physics*, not in *Chemistry*. Chemistry deals with such changes only incidentally.

The molecules (small, invisible particles) of a solid move with difficulty upon each other. The molecules of a liquid move readily upon each other, so that the liquid assumes the shape of the vessel holding it. The molecules of gas have an apparent repulsion for each other, so that a gas, regardless of its specific gravity (*i. e.* whether *light* or *heavy*), escapes from an open vessel and diffuses itself throughout the surrounding space.

We learn many things incidentally about solids and liquids before studying either Physics or Chemistry. We know comparatively little about gases, except about the gaseous ocean of air at the bottom of which we live. To the chemist, however, the gas is in many respects the simplest state of matter and the most convenient for him to examine critically.

CHAPTER II.

The **Atomic Theory** divides matter into:—

1. Mass.—Any portion of matter *appreciable by the senses*.

2. Molecule.—The smallest particle of matter that can take part in a mere physical change. It may exist alone.

3. Atom.—The smallest particle of matter that can take part in a chemical change. An atom does not exist alone. Atoms compose molecules: *i.e.*, two or more atoms make a molecule.

Chemistry treats of the atomic condition of matter and especially of atomic changes.

It will be inferred from the definitions that a *mass* may be very large or exceedingly small, also, that the molecule and the atom are not visible even with the aid of the most powerful microscope, otherwise *they* would be "appreciable by the senses."

Chemistry treats of more subtle changes than physics. If the molecule is not broken up and the *atoms* set free to form new combinations, it matters not how violent, or how wonderful the change may be, it is purely *physical* and in no sense chemical.

Of course, atoms "exist alone" during the instant of chemical change. One atom may rarely make a molecule. At this stage, however, the pupil should not trouble himself with exceptions.

NOTE.—We know that there are masses and molecules, but we do not know that there is any such thing as an atom. More than this we do not care whether there is or not. The atom is to chemistry what the x, or unknown quantity, is to algebra. It enables us to accomplish results which otherwise would be impossible. The Atomic Theory is as useful in the study of **chemistry** as the Arabic numerals are in the study of arithmetic.

CHAPTER III.

An **Element** is a substance whose molecules contain atoms of one kind only; therefore it cannot be separated into two or more different kinds of substances. Ex., gold, lead, hydrogen.

A **binary** compound is a substance which has *two* different kinds of atoms in its molecule, and therefore can be separated into two different kinds of substances. Ex., water, common salt.

A molecule of hydrogen may be represented thus $\boxed{\text{H H}}$ in which each H represents an atom of hydrogen and the boundary line simply the fact that the two atoms are bound together by chemical bonds into one molecule.

It is well to remember that we can only *represent* a point on the board, or upon paper, we cannot make one. We only *represent* lines, we cannot make them. The "point" on the board is infinitely too large for a real point. So the H above is too large to represent *with any suggestiveness as to size* an atom of hydrogen. Let the pupil imagine in place of the two H's in the molecule two infinitesimally small particles of hydrogen side by side. These are precisely alike; are mysteriously held together by some peculiar law allied to gravitation, and act in most cases, *i. e.* in all physical cases, as one particle. The two atoms taken together (the one molecule of hydrogen) must be much too small to be seen even with a microscope, and there must be many millions of molecules in a very small vessel full of hydrogen.

A molecule of water may be represented thus $\boxed{\text{HOH}}$ or more briefly, thus $\boxed{H_2O}$ or still more briefly by omitting the boundary line, thus H_2O. This means that in a molecule of water there are two atoms of hydrogen (precisely alike) and one atom (unlike the other two) of oxygen.

An attentive student will readily grasp the condition of matter which the Atomic Theory supposes, both as to the elements and as to binary compounds. The immense value of the theory will be seen as it is developed into practical results in the following chapters.

Practically the representation H_2O means that *two* parts *by volume* of hydrogen unite with *one* part *by volume* of oxygen to form the binary compound which we call water. (Take this for granted now; we'll prove it by and by. See WATER, index.) Thus, two *gases* unite to form a liquid. But this is a chemical change, because the atoms of the molecules of hydrogen and of oxygen are disturbed, their molecules being broken up to form new molecules of a *different* substance, water. The change may be represented thus:—

$$[HH] \ [HH] + [OO] = [H_2O] \ [H_2O]$$

This means that two molecules of hydrogen and one molecule of oxygen break up into separate atoms and then instantaneously reunite into two molecules of water.

The atomic change (beginning at the instant when the molecules are broken up) may be written thus:—

$$H_2 \quad + \quad O \quad = \quad H_2O$$

Two atoms of hydrogen   One atom of oxygen   One molecule of water

Chemical changes are called **Reactions.** For all ordinary purposes the atomic reaction is correct. As it is not nearly so difficult as the molecular reaction (first above) it alone will be used in this book.

There are about *sixty-seven* elements known, and these may be considered the alphabet of chemistry. From these all chemical compounds are formed, as words from letters.

CHAPTER IV.

Atoms of different elements differ in three essential respects:—

1. In **weight**.
2. In **quality**.
3. In **strength**.

The **First Difference** needs no explanation. When we say that atoms differ in weight, we mean that they differ in weight. (Atoms of the same element have always the same weight.)

The **Second Difference** needs explanation. The quality of meat may be determined *by eating* it, and the quality is said to be *good* or *bad*. The quality of cloth may be told *by wearing* it, and the quality of cloth is also said to be good or bad, as the case may be.

The quality of an atom is determined by **electricity,** and the atom is said to be, not *good* or *bad*, but **positive** or **negative.**

If a current of electricity from two or more of Bunsen's quart cups be passed through the binary compound water, the water will be decomposed and bubbles of gas will appear at each pole. If the gas from the positive pole be collected (see Fig. No. 1) and tested, it will prove to be oxygen. If the gas from the negative pole be collected and tested, it will prove to be hydrogen and will have twice the volume of the oxygen.

NOTE.—The water should be acidulated slightly with sulphuric acid. The hydrogen will always have a little more than twice the volume of the oxygen, because the liberated oxygen is more soluble in (the remaining) water than the hydrogen. The pupil may learn right here that *a gas can be dissolved in water just as well as a solid.* The nature of a mere solution will be explained hereafter. [See Chap. XV.]

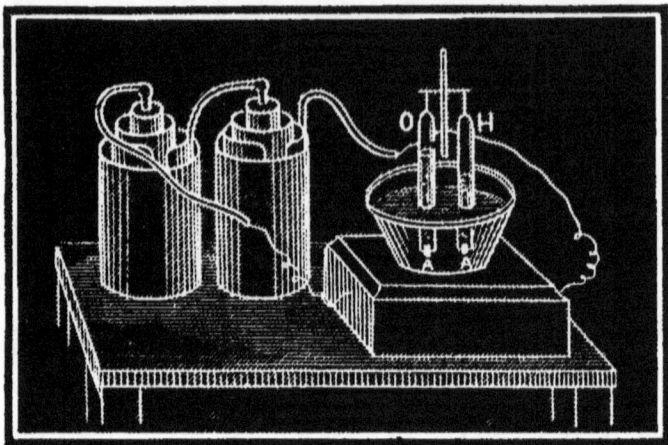

Fig. 1. A A—Platinum Ends (poles, or electrodes).

The law of electricity being that "*like electricities repel each other and unlike attract*"—as oxygen goes to the positive pole, it is *negative* to hydrogen, and as hydrogen goes to the negative pole, it is *positive* to oxygen.

Thus, by means of a battery acting upon their compounds, the elements may be arranged with reference to their "quality"—but an atom of an element is always positive or negative, not absolutely, but relatively.

For example, if we arrange in line sixty-seven boys from north to south, the first boy would be a *north* boy to any other. The second boy would be a south boy compared with the *first*, but a north boy compared with the *third*. The tenth boy would be a south boy compared with the fourth, but a north boy compared with the fifteenth. Any boy would be a south boy to all boys north of himself, but a north boy to all boys south of himself.

Thus, the elements are arranged in line according to their "quality," oxygen standing first, being most negative. (See Reference Table No. 1.) This difference in "quality" is of the utmost importance in chemistry.

The **Third Difference** may be explained by an illustration.

If one man can hold a 100-lb. weight, we may call his strength *one*. Then, if another man can hold two 100-lb. weights, his strength would be *two*, and it would take two of the first kind of men to match one of the second kind. If a third man can hold three 100-lb. weights, his

THEORETICAL CHEMISTRY. 15

strength would be *three*, and it would take three of the first kind of men to match one of the third. But how shall we match the second kind of men and the third kind? Evidently, three of the second kind would match two of the third kind. If a fourth man can hold four 100-lb. weights, his strength will be *four*; etc.

The strength of atoms is measured, not by 100-lb. weights, but by the strength of hydrogen atoms. The strength of the hydrogen atom is taken as *one*. The strength of those elements whose atoms each require one atom of hydrogen to match them is *one*; of those elements whose atoms each require two atoms of hydrogen to match them, the strength is *two*; of those whose atoms require three atoms of hydrogen, the strength is *three*, etc.

These elements are called respectively monads (1), dyads (2), triads (3), tetrads (4), pentads (5), hexads (6), and heptads (7). This strength of the atoms is often expressed adjectively by the terms, univalent (1), bivalent (2), trivalent (3), quadrivalent (4), pentivalent (5), etc.

CHAPTER V.

The names of the elements are abbreviated in chemical language. O is the symbol for oxygen, S for sulphur, Sb for antimony (Latin, *stibium*), etc. The dictionary will give the Latin name from which a number of the symbols are derived.

The following **Reference Table** exhibits the symbols of the most important elements and the *three essential differences* of their atoms:—

REFERENCE TABLE NO. 1.

SYMBOL.	QUALITY. Shown by order of names	ATOMIC WEIGHT.	STRENGTH.
	Negative End.		
O	Oxygen	16	2
S	Sulphur	32	2
N	Nitrogen	14	3
F	Fluorine	19	1
Cl	Chlorine	35.5	1
Br	Bromine	80	1
I	Iodine	127	1
CN	Cyanogen*	26	1
Se	Selenium	79	2
P	Phosphorus	31	5—(3)
As	Arsenicum	75	3—(5)
Cr	Chromium	52.5	2
B	Boron	11	3
C	Carbon	12	4—(2)
Sb	Antimony	122	3—(5)
Si	Silicon	28	4
H	**HYDROGEN**	1	1
Au	Gold	196.6	3—(1)
Pt	Platinum	197	4—(2)
Hg	Mercury	200	2 (Hg$_2$ a dyad)
Ag	Silver	108	1
Cu	Copper	63.5	2 (Cu$_2$ a dyad)
Bi	Bismuth	210	3
Sn	Tin	118	4—(2)
Pb	Lead	207	2—(4)
Co	Cobalt	59	2
Ni	Nickel	59	2
Fe	Iron	56	2 (Fe$_2$ a hexad)
Zn	Zinc	65	2
Mn	Manganese	55	2—(4)
Al	Aluminum	27.5	Al$_2$ a hexad
Mg	Magnesium	24	2
Ca	Calcium	40	2
Sr	Strontium	87.5	2
Ba	Barium	137	2
Na	Sodium	23	1
K	Potassium	39	1
H$_4$N	Ammonium*	18	1
	Positive End.		

[See Chap. VII. for explanation of this column.]

Above. / Below.

*Not elements. (See Chap. VI.)

CHAPTER VI.

A **binary compound** is named by placing the positive element first and changing the ending of the negative into **ide**.

EXAMPLES.

Formula. Name.

Na Cl = sodium chlor**ide**.
K_2 O = potassium ox**ide**.

It will be noticed that sodium and chlorine are both monads (see strength in Reference Table No. 1), and therefore it requires *one* atom of each to match the other in the molecule, as in the first example. In the second example, potassium is a monad (see TABLE), but oxygen is a dyad, therefore it takes *two* atoms of potassium to match *one* of oxygen in the molecule.

Again, in putting dyads and triads together, we must take *three dyads* to match *two triads* in the molecule, a strength of two times three equaling a strength of *three* times *two*.

EXAMPLE.

$As_2 S_3$ = arsenicum sulphide.

Again, two dyads must be taken to match one tetrad.

EXAMPLE.

$C O_2$ = carbon oxide.

Aluminum is peculiar. A single atom is never found in any molecule, but two atoms together have a strength of six.

EXAMPLE.

$Al_2 Cl_6$ = aluminum chloride.

Five dyads must be taken to match two pentads.

EXAMPLE.

$P_2 S_5$ = phosphorus sulphide.

NOTE.—Just as we sometimes say "the father of Mary," instead of "Mary's father," the older chemists say "sulphide of phosphorus," instead of "phosphorus sulphide." They also express the same by "sulph*uret* of phosphorus," or "sulphuretted phosphorus."

Atoms of two or more elements bound together by chemical bonds so closely as to act as one atom in the formation of compounds, form a **Compound Radical**.

Two very important compound radicals are inserted in the Reference Table and linked with the elements with which they are closely allied. Their compounds with a single element are considered and named as binaries, though they contain *three* different kinds of atoms.

EXAMPLES.

K $\overline{CN}$ = potassium cyanide.

$(\overline{H_4 N})_2 S$ = ammonium sulphide.

$\overline{H_4 N}$ $\overline{CN}$ = ammonium cyanide.

Fig. 2

NOTE.—The pupil should write the formulas and names of a great many binary compounds, putting the atoms together according to the strength in the Reference Table. Be careful that the multiplications make the positives match in strength the negatives, as in the examples. It does not matter if many of the compounds are merely theoretical. It is, however, a great gain at this point to have as many binaries *as combine according to the first strength given in the Table*, shown to the scholars. For instance, a substance might be shown and the class told that it was a compound of sulphur and sodium. They should then all write labels for the bottle containing it, giving formula and name, as in Fig. 2.

CHAPTER VII.

Ic and Ous Binaries.

These may be introduced by an illustration: In one of our Eastern townships lived a man who was afflicted with periodic insanity. When in his right mind (ordinarily), he had the strength of his brother. He could be called a *monad*. In one of his insane fits he carried three men upon his back over a gate five boards high. He became a very decided *triad*, you see.

Now, the **Reference Table No. 1** gives the "strength" of chlorine *one*, *i. e.*, as a monad—but sometimes it acts with a strength of three, *i. e.*, as a triad (sometimes as a pentad, or even as a heptad).

Carbon is given a strength of four, and this it ordinarily has—but sometimes it acts with a strength of only *two*. Thus, it forms two binary compounds with oxygen, CO_2 and CO. Evidently, if we say carbon oxide, we shall not know which is meant, because the name may apply to either.

As a rule, an atom with an *even* strength never has an *odd* strength, also, an atom with an *odd* strength never has an *even* strength. The strength increases or decreases by *twos*. This will be noticed as we proceed.

The column in parenthesis in Table under STRENGTH, includes all the variation that beginners will need for reference in writing binaries.

We must invent some way to distinguish the different compounds, when an element acts with different strengths.

When the positive takes **more** of the negative, it has the ending **ic**, when it takes **less** of the negative, it has the ending **ous**.

EXAMPLES.

CO_2 = carbon**ic** oxide.
CO = carbon**ous** oxide.

When the positive takes *more* of the negative than in the *ic* compound, it has the prefix *per* (from *hyper* = more); when it takes *less* of the negative, than in the *ous* compound, it takes the prefix *hypo* (under).

EXAMPLES.

$Cl_2 O$ = *hypo*-chlor*ous* oxide.	(Cl a monad)
$Cl_2 O_3$ = chlor*ous* oxide.	(Cl a triad)
$Cl_2 O_5$ = chlor*ic* oxide.	(Cl a pentad)
$Cl_2 O_7$ = *per*-chlor*ic* oxide.	(Cl a heptad)

NOTE.—*Per* and *hypo* are rarely prefixed to the negative instead of to the positive. Few elements form *hypo-* and *per* binaries. and the pupil will be troubled very little with them. They are given here so that if, in the larger text-books, he sees *hypo-* and *per-*binaries mentioned, he may have some idea of what is meant.

The scholar should here solve many problems, such as the following:—

1. Put together sulphur and antimony to form two compounds. giving antimony a strength in the first compound *as in the Table*, and in the second compound a strength as in the parenthesis. Name.

Ans. $Sb_2 S_3$ = antimon*ous* sulphide.
$Sb_2 S_5$ = antimon*ic* sulphide.

2. Put together iodine and mercury, giving mercury a strength, first, as in Table; second, as in the parenthesis. Name.

Ans. $Hg I_2$ = merc*uric* iodide.
$Hg_2 I_2$ = mércur*ous* iodide.

NOTE.—In this last compound, mercury *seems* to be a monad, *i. e.*, it *seems* to change from the *even* to the *odd* strength. A few of the other elements do the same thing, as you will see. For practical purposes, this last formula has sometimes been written $Hg I$ = mercur*ous* iodide, but it is better to write as above.

The *ic* and *ous* compounds of the same elements often differ very much in physical and chemical properties. You will see, by looking at the samples from the laboratory, that mercur*ic* iodide is *red*, while mercur*ous* iodide is *green*. Again, carbon*ic* oxide is *not* poisonous, while carbon*ous* oxide *is* poisonous.

Notice that for gold, copper, tin, lead, and iron, the adjectives (from Latin) aurous, cuprous, stannous, plumbous, and ferrous, respectively, are used in one compound, and auric, cupric, etc., in the other.

A binary *may* be named by prefixing the Greek numerals (*mon, di, tri, tetra, etc*). In all cases where a mistake would be likely to occur, this very exact method is used.

EXAMPLES.

CO = carbon monoxide. (*ous.*)
CO_2 = carbon dioxide. (*ic.*)
Fe_2O_3 = di-ferric trioxide. (*ic.*)

NOTE.—The older chemists used, as a rule, *per* and *proto* for *ic* and *ous* respectively, as:—

FeO = *proto*xide of iron, instead of ferrous oxide.
Fe_2O_3 = *per*oxide of iron, instead of ferric oxide.

Instead of *ous*, the prefix *sub* was also used, as: Hg_2Cl_2 = *sub*chloride of mercury.

Compounds, in which there were *two* of the positive to *three* of the negative, often took the prefix *sesqui* (one and one-half), as:—
Fe_2O_3 = sesquioxide of iron.

There is still another name which the unfortunate druggist must learn, a Latin name with which he labels his bottles. (See Chap. XIII., NOTE.)

Write the names of the following, using *ic* and *ous* in the first three columns and the Greek prefixes in the last column:—

As_2O_3 =	$AuCl_3$ =	Sb_2O_5 =	MnO_2 =
As_2O_5 =	Fe_2Cl_6 =	$PtCl_4$ =	CO_2 =
SnS_2 =	Hg_2Cl_2 =	Sb_2S_3 =	PCl_5 =
SnS =	$AuCl$ =	$PtBr_2$ =	PCl_3 =
P_2O_5 =	Cu_2O =	CO =	Fe_2S_3 =
P_2O_3 =	CuO =	FeS =	CO =
$HgCl_2$ =	$Hg2CN$ =	$PbBr_4$ =	CS_2 =
HgS =	PbI_2 =	CuS =	PbO =

CHAPTER VIII.

Inspection of the following questions and the methods of solution will reveal the great value of the Atomic Theory to the chemist, and, indeed, to the world of industry.

1. In 116 kilograms* of mercuric sulphide (Hg S) how much mercury?

$$Hg = 200 \text{ atomic weight (see Table).}$$
$$S = 32 \quad `` \quad ``$$
$$\overline{Hg\,S = 232 \text{ molecular weight.}}$$

232 kgs. of Hg S $\overset{\text{corresponds to}}{=}$ 200 kgs. of Hg.
1 " " = $\frac{1}{232}$ of 200 kgs. of Hg.
116 " " = $\frac{116}{232}$ of 200 " "
$\frac{116}{232}$ of 200 = 100 kgs. of Hg *Ans.*

2. How much lead chloride (Pb Cl$_2$) could be made from 50 grams of lead?

$$Pb = 207 \text{ at. wt.}$$
$$Cl_2 = 71 \quad ``$$
$$\overline{Pb\,Cl_2 = 278 \text{ mol. wt.}}$$

207 Pb = 278 Pb Cl$_2$
1 " = $\frac{1}{207}$ of 278 Pb Cl$_2$
50 " = $\frac{50}{207}$ of 278 " = $67\frac{31}{207}$ grams. *Ans.*

It will be noticed that there are two distinct kinds of questions. The first gives the weight of the binary and requires the weight of the

*See metric system, Index.

element The second gives the weight of the element and requires the weight of the binary. In the first class of questions of course, the answer is *less* than the given weight. In the second class the answer is *more* than the given weight. After obtaining the molecular weight by the addition of the atomic weights, set in the left hand number of the first equation the weight (atomic or molecular) of the *given* quantity as in the example.

3. From one metric ton of the iron ore hematite ($Fe_2 O_3$, ferric oxide), how many kilograms of iron could be obtained, provided the hematite contained 25 per cent. of earthy impurities, or waste?

$$1 \text{ M. T.} = 1000 \text{ kgs.}$$
25 per cent. waste leaves 75 per cent.
$$\overline{750 \text{ kgs. of pure ore.}}$$

$$Fe_2 = 112 \text{ at. wt.}$$
$$O_3 = 48 \text{ ``}$$
$$\overline{Fe_2 O_3 = 160 \text{ mol. wt.}}$$

$160 \ Fe_2 O_3 = 112 \ Fe$
$1 \text{ ``} = \frac{1}{160} \text{ of } 112 \ Fe$
$750 \text{ ``} = \frac{750}{160} \text{ of } 112 \ Fe = 525 \text{ kgs. iron.} \quad Ans.$

NOTE.—The pupil should perform very many problems similar to the above. To show one common process of getting the element from the ore, heat some lead oxide (litharge) on charcoal (carbon) in the blowpipe flame. The carbon takes the oxygen from the lead, forming carbonic oxide ($C O_2$) and leaves the lead *free*, *i. e.*, not combined with any other element (see Exp. 50).

4. How much lead in 100 kgs. of lead oxide (Pb O)? *Ans.* $92\frac{184}{223}$.

5. One M. T. of lead would make how many kilograms of litharge?
    Ans. $1077\frac{61}{207}$.

6. How much silver in 50 kgs. of silver chloride?

7. How much silver chloride must be taken to obtain from it 50 kgs. of silver?

8. How much mercury would be required to make 150 kgs. of vermilion (mercuric sulphide)?

9. How much lead in one metric ton of plumbous chloride?

10. How much gold in 500 grams of auric chloride?

CHAPTER IX.

A **ternary compound** is one having *three* different kinds of atoms in its molecule, and therefore can be separated into three different kinds of substances.

Most ternaries contain oxygen as a *connecting* element; it is therefore omitted in the name. It is *understood* to be the connecting element, unless otherwise mentioned (see Sulph-Salts, Index). It is not omitted in the formula.

A ternary is named by placing the positive first and (the O being omitted) the negative last, with the ending changed into **ate**.

EXAMPLES.

$K\,Cl\,O_3$ = potassium chlor**ate**.
$H_2\,SO_4$ = hydrogen sulph**ate**.

As in binaries, we have different compounds of the same *three* elements, and so must have different names.

When the O is *less* (relatively to the negative) than in the **ate** compound, the negative takes the ending **ite**.

EXAMPLES.

$K\,Cl\,O_3$ = potassium chlor**ate**.
$K\,Cl\,O_2$ = potassium chlor**ite**.

Rarely the O may be *less* than in the *ite* compound, when *hypo......ite* is used. Sometimes the O is *more* than in the *ate* compound, when *per......ate* is used.

EXAMPLES.

$K\,Cl\,O$ = potassium *hypo*-chlor*ite*.
$K\,Cl\,O_2$ = potassium chlor*ite*.
$K\,Cl\,O_3$ = potassium chlor*ate*.
$K\,Cl\,O_4$ = potassium *per*-chlor*ate*.

THEORETICAL CHEMISTRY. 25

As in binaries, the *hypo-* and *per-*ternaries are very few and will trouble the student very little. The **ite** compounds are also few in comparison with the **ate**. This will be a good rule for beginners: "*Call every ternary an* ate *unless you have reason to call it an* ite."

Name the following:—

$H_3 PO_4 = ?$
$K NO_3 =$
$Ca\ 2\ HO =$

$Mg\ SO_4 =$ } Which is the *ate* and
$Mg\ SO_3 =$ } which the *ite* compound?
$Ca_3\ 2\ PO_4 =$

NOTE.—Don't ask why the atoms in the above are matched or multiplied as they are. You will not understand this till you have completed Chap. XII.

CHAPTER X.

There are three great classes of ternaries, with which the scholar should early become familiar, viz.:—**acids, bases,** and **salts.**

Acids are generally **sour,** and turn *blue* vegetable colors (such as litmus) **red.**

Bases (those that are soluble in water are called **alkalies**) turn *red* litmus paper **blue.**

Acids and bases are chemical opposites. They attack and destroy each other, forming **salts** (and water). This power of forming a *salt* with its opposites is the true test for an acid or a base. The test with litmus paper is a very good one and usually answers.

NOTE.—The pupil should here test a number of acids and bases with litmus paper. Of course, acids, bases, and salts may exist in either of the *three* physical states: solid, liquid, or gaseous. Solid or gaseous acids and bases must be dissolved in water before testing, or the litmus paper wet (which is the same thing).

Acids, bases, and salts are said to be formed on the **water-type,** thus:—

$\boxed{\text{H H O}}$ = molecule of water.

$\boxed{\text{H, a \textbf{negative} element and O}}$ = a molecule of an acid.

$\boxed{\text{A \textbf{positive} element. H and O}}$ = a molecule of a base.

$\boxed{\text{A \textbf{positive} element, a \textbf{negative} element and O}}$ = a molecule of a salt.

In the above *water-type*, by a negative element is meant one **negative to hydrogen,** and by a positive element one **positive to hydrogen.**

In the Reference Table, if the element is above hydrogen, it is *negative* in forming acids, bases, or salts; if below hydrogen, it is *positive*.

Write the name of the following, and mark as acid, base, or salt. (Consult Table No. 1. A large figure multiplies all atoms that follow it.)

$\overset{+\ -}{\text{K Cl O}_3}$ = potassium chlorate = salt.

$\overset{-}{\text{H}_2\text{ S O}_4}$ = hydrogen sulphate = acid.

$\overset{+}{\text{Ca 2 HO}}$ = calcium hydrate = base.

$Na_2 SO_4$ = ?	$(H_4 N)_2 SO_4$ =	$Na\ HO$ =	$Ba\ 2\ HO$ =
$H\ NO_3$ =	$H_2 SO_3$ =	$Mg_3\ 2\ PO_4$ =	$Pb\ Cr\ O_4$ =
$K\ NO_3$ =	$Ag_3\ As\ O_4$ =	$Na\ Cl\ O_3$ =	$H_3\ BO_3$ =

NOTE.—The division into *positive* and *negative* elements is not always made at hydrogen. Thus, zinc is *usually* positive in forming by the water-type, and $\overset{+}{\text{Zn 2 HO}}$ zinc hydrate = base—but *rarely,* when in presence of a stronger positive element, as potassium: $\overset{+}{\text{Zn 2 HO}}$ zinc hydrate becomes (or may be considered) $H_2\ Zn\ O_2$ = hydrogen zincate = an acid; and we have the salt $\overset{+\ -}{\text{K}_2\ \text{Zn O}_2}$ = potassium zincate, in which Zn is negative not to H but to K. So chromium *usually* by the water-type acts as a negative element, and $\overset{-}{\text{H}_2\ \text{Cr O}_4}$ = hydrogen chromate = an acid, but rarely chromium acts as a positive element, and we have $\overset{+}{Cr_2}$ 6 HO = chromium hydrate = a base. The pupil at this stage, however, should not attempt to deal with exceptions, but should treat the *rule* given as though it were absolute, and should consider all elements above hydrogen as negative and all elements below hydrogen as positive in the formation of acids, bases, and salts. After deciding from the formula, test acids and bases by litmus paper, and thus prove the rule. This water type should be so thoroughly mastered that, having *the Reference Table before you*, you can tell at a glance, on seeing the formula, whether the ternary is an acid, base, or salt.

CHAPTER XI

It will be noticed that in the Reference Table four negative elements and one compound radical are linked together. These elements are called the **haloid elements** (or halogens = salt-forming), because they form salts (and acids) *without oxygen*, *i. e.*, they form **binary salts and acids.**

EXAMPLES.

$H \overset{-}{Cl}$ = hydrogen chloride = a binary acid.

$\overset{+}{Mg} \overset{-}{Cl_2}$ = magnesium chloride = a binary salt.

These salts and acids may be referred to the water-type by counting in the missing oxygen, thus $H \overset{-}{Cl}$ = **hydrogen, a neg.** and the missing O = an acid.

Write the name, and mark as acid, base, or salt, the following:—

$\overset{+}{K_2} \overset{-}{SO_4}$ = potassium sulphate = salt.

$\overset{+}{K} \overset{-}{CN}$ = potassium cyanide = binary salt.

$Na_2 S$ = sodium sulphide = (neither).

$\overset{+}{H_4N} \overset{-}{NO_3}$ = ammonium nitrate = salt.

H I = ?	Ca Cl$_2$ =	Mg 2 CN =	Mg CO$_3$ =
K$_2$ CO$_3$ =	K Br =	Ba 2 Cl O$_3$ =	(H$_4$N)$_2$ CO$_3$ =
H$_4$N HO =	H$_3$ PO$_4$ =	H$_2$ SO$_3$ =	Ag Cl =
Mg$_3$ 2 PO$_4$ =	Mg 2 HO =	Mg SO$_4$ =	H$_4$ Si O$_4$ =

NOTE.—The *third example* above teaches us that there are many binaries which are not to be classed as acids, bases, or salts. Only those binaries containing the "salt-forming" elements and radical linked in Table No. 1, are to be thus classified. Evidently there can be no binary bases.

CHAPTER XII.

The following **Reference Table No. 2** will be found a great aid in writing formulas of ternaries. It is to be used in connection with Table No. 1, the negative "**groupings**" in No. 2, being used with the positive (to H) elements in No. 1, and the positive groupings (all radicals) of No. 2, with either the negative elements of No. 1, or the negative groupings of No. 2. The positive groupings in No. 2, being radicals, unite with a single element to form a *binary*, while the negative groupings in No. 2, not being radicals (in the same sense), unite with a single element to form a *ternary*.

EXAMPLE.

(C$_2$ H$_5$)$_2$ O = ethyl ox*ide* (common ether) = a binary; but

Mg CO$_3$ = magnesium carbon*ate* = a ternary; and

K HO = potassium hydr*ate* = a ternary.

THEORETICAL CHEMISTRY. 29

REFERENCE TABLE NO. 2.

GROUPINGS.

NEGATIVE.

POSITIVE.

UNIVALENT OR MONAD.
- HO = hydrate.
- NO_3 = nitrate.
- $Cl\, O_3$ = chlorate
- $C_2H_3O_2$ = acetate
- $\begin{cases} C_{18}H_{35}O_2 = \text{stearate} \\ C_{16}H_{31}O_2 = \text{palmitate} \\ C_{18}H_{33}O_2 = \text{oleate} \end{cases}$ (in fats)

(Radicals)
- H_4N = ammonium
- C_2H_5 = ethyl
- C_6H_5 = phenyl
- CH_3 = methyl
- C_5H_{11} = amyl

BIVALENT OR DYAD.
- SO_4 = sulphate
- SO_3 = sulphite
- CO_3 = carbonate
- C_2O_4 = oxalate
- $C_4H_4O_6$ = tartrate
- $Cr\, O_4$ = chromate
- $Se\, O_4$ = selenate

TRIVALENT OR TRIAD.
- PO_4 = phosphate
- $As\, O_4$ = arsenate
- $As\, O_3$ = arsenite
- $Sb\, O_4$ = antimonate
- $B\, O_3$ = borate
- $C_6H_5O_7$ = citrate.

C_3H_5 = glyceryl (in fats)

Quadrivalent or Tetrad.
- $Si\, O_4$ = silicate
- P_2O_7 = pyrophosphate

It has probably been noticed that in the examples given in the previous chapters, all *hydrates* contain HO, which acts as a monad with reference to the elements that go with it, also, that all sulphates contain the dyad grouping SO_4.

To write the formula of any substance, whose *name* is given, as potassium carbonate, we first find the carbonate grouping in Table No. 2, and write it thus, $\overline{CO_3}''$, indicating for convenience its strength by the *two* marks above. In Table No. 1 we find K has a strength of *one;* placing this before the carbonate grouping, we have $K'\overline{CO_3}''$. But it takes two monads to match one dyad, therefore we must multiply K by two, and we have $K_2\overline{CO_3}$ for the formula required.

Write the formula for magnesium phosphate:—

phosphate grouping = $\overline{PO_4}'''$
magnesium = Mg'';

As it takes *three* dyads to match *two* triads, we have Mg_3 2 $\overline{PO_4}$ for the required formula.

NOTE 1.—The above Table contains only the most common groupings. There are phosphate groupings other than the two mentioned; also other borate, sulphate, and silicate groupings, etc. For rarer groupings see "Table No. 2, continued." The number of radicals, both negative and positive, is countless. It is well for beginners to put a vinculum above the groupings and radicals until they are familiar with the method of matching them.

NOTE 2.—H, united with the hydrate grouping, gives H $\overline{HO}$ or H_2O = hydrogen oxide, a binary. The grouping $\overline{HO}$ is often considered a compound radical (hydroxyl) and its compound with an element is sometimes named as a binary. Ex: K $\overline{HO}$ = potassium hydroxide, instead of as in third example above.

CHAPTER XIII.

Write formulas for the following, and mark as *acid*, *base*, or *salt:*—
  potassium arsenate = K_3AsO_4 = salt.
  calcium acetate = $Ca\ 2\ C_2H_3O_2$ = salt.
  hydrogen nitrate = HNO_3 = acid.
  magnesium hydrate = $Mg\ 2\ HO$ = base.

hydrogen silicate =   barium phosphate =
calcium oxalate =   lead chromate
sodium carbonate =   potassium arsenate =
calcium phosphate =   ethyl hydrate (common alcohol) =
hydrogen acetate =   ammonium oxalate =
sodium hydrate =   hydrogen tartrate =
lead carbonate =   glyceryl hydrate (glycerine) =
magnesium phosphate =   barium nitrate =
hydrogen citrate =   silver arsenite =

NOTE.—Notice that in negative groupings containing three or more elements, the hydrogen is not counted in applying the water-type. See calcium acetate above.

As there is in acids but one element unknown (or variable), the acids are often called by *pet* names, using this element as an adjective; thus,

HNO_3 = nit*ric* acid, instead of hydrogen nit*rate*.
H_2SO_4 = sulphu*ric* acid, instead of hydrogen sulph*ate*.
H_2SO_3 = sulphur*ous* acid, instead of hydrogen sulph*ite*.

In the *pet* name of binary acids both elements are used; as HCl = hydrochloric acid (or chlorohydric), instead of hydrogen chloride. (H Cl has still another pet name used in commerce, a commercial name, muriatic acid.) As you should not call a stranger by his pet name, so it is much better for you not to call any chemical compound by its pet name till you know its composition thoroughly and its chemical (systematic) name.

NOTE.—Most chemical compounds have one or more pet names, used in commerce, by miners, by workmen in the arts, by mineralogists, or by pharmacists. In works on chemistry these names are often inserted after the chemical name (or *vice versa*). The druggist must learn at least three different names for nearly all substances. For example, a boy calls for "copperas." The druggist thinks "iron sulphate" and takes it from a bottle labeled, in Latin, "*Ferri Sulphas.*" The older chemists say sulphate of copper, of magnesia, of lime, of soda, of potassa (or potash), for respectively, copper, magnesium, calcium, sodium, and potassium sulphate.

If the molecular composition of the acids has been mastered, they may be called by their pet names hereafter. Notice that the formulas for all acids begin with H, while formulas for all bases end in the grouping HO.

Write formulas for the following:—

phosphoric acid   acetic acid
chromic acid   boracic acid
citric acid   pyrophosphoric acid
hydrofluoric acid   sulphurous acid

Inspection of the following questions will show that the methods of solution are the same, whether the compound is a binary or a ternary.

1. In 580 kgs. of the iron ore, ferrous carbonate ($Fe\ CO_3$ spathic iron), how much iron?

$Fe = 56$ at. wt. $116\ Fe\ CO_3 = 56\ Fe$
$C = 12$ " 1 " $= \frac{1}{116}$ of $56\ Fe$,
$O_3 = 48$ " 580 kgs. " $= \frac{580}{116}$ of 56 kgs. Fe; $=$
_____
$Fe\ CO_3 = 116$ mol. wt. 280 kgs.—*Ans.*

2. How much zinc sulphate could be made from 130 kgs. of Zn?

$Zn = 65$ $65\ Zn = 161\ Zn\ SO_4$
$S = 32$ $1\ Zn = \frac{1}{65}$ of $161\ Zn\ SO_4$
$O_4 = 64$ 130 kgs. $Zn = \frac{130}{65}$ of 161 kgs. $Zn\ SO_4$
_____
$Zn\ SO_4 = 161$ 322 kgs.—*Ans.*

3. In 100 kgs. of potassium arsenate how much arsenicum?

4. In 150 gms. of mercuric (Hg = dyad) nitrate, how much mercury?

5. In 75 gms. of mercur*ous* (Hg_2 = dyad) nitrate, how much mercury?

6. How much lead carbonate (white lead) could be made from 50 kgs. of lead?

CHAPTER XIV.

We have seen that chemical changes are called **reactions**. There are various classes of reactions, of which the simpler should be thoroughly mastered by beginners, and the more complex let severely alone.

CLASS 1.

Reaction by **Direct Union** (or **Separation**).

Fig. 3.

EXPERIMENT. 1.—Heat a small quantity of sulphur well mixed with fine copper fillings on a broken test-tube or other piece of glass; a reaction takes place and copper sulph*ide* is formed.

Reaction (atomic): $\underset{\substack{\text{copper}\\(\text{red})}}{\text{Cu}} + \underset{\substack{\text{sulphur}\\(\text{yellow})}}{\text{S}} =$
$\underset{\substack{\text{copper sulphide}\\(\text{black})}}{\text{Cu S}}$

EXP. 2.—In a test-tube of hard glass place a small quantity of mercuric oxide (red) and close by rubber cork through which passes a fine **glass tube** connected to rubber tubing (Fig. 3). Place mouth of tube below the surface of water and heat test-tube to dull redness. The oxygen separates from the mercury and escapes bubbling through the water, while the mercury condenses in a ring upon the colder part of the test-tube.

Reaction: $\underset{\text{red solid}}{\text{Hg O}} = \underset{\text{liquid}}{\text{Hg}} + \underset{\substack{\text{invisible}\\\text{gas}}}{\text{O}}$

Exp. 3.—Burn a small piece of magnesium ribbon in the air; the oxygen of the air unites with the magnesium, forming magnesium oxide.

Reaction: $\underset{\text{magnesium}}{Mg} + \underset{\text{oxygen}}{O} = \underset{\text{magnesium oxide}}{MgO}$

1. How much MgO could be made by burning 30 gms. of Mg?

2. If you make 80 gms. of MgO, how much Mg must you take?

Air is composed of *one* part by volume of the gas oxygen and about *four* parts by volume of the gas nitrogen (with traces of carbonic oxide and vapor of water, etc.). Burning, or **combustion,** is, in general, the *rapid* union of a substance with oxygen. The temperature at which the substance takes fire, *i. e.*, unites *rapidly* with the oxygen of the air, is called the **igniting point** (*i. e.*, kindling point). Of course, the product of the burning will be an **oxide.**

Exp. 4.—Burn some sulphur in a bottle containing a small quantity of water. (See Fig. 13 and Exp. 23. S in burning always acts as a tetrad.)

Reaction (a): $S + O_2 = SO_2$ (a gas)

Close the mouth of the bottle and shake;

Reaction (b): $SO_2 + H_2O = H_2SO_3$ (an acid)

Test for the acid by litmus paper.

Exp. 5.—Scrape some fine powder from a piece of quicklime into a test-tube of water;

Reaction: $\underset{\text{quicklime}}{CaO} + H_2O = \underset{\substack{\text{water-slaked lime,} \\ \text{a soft solid, part} \\ \text{of which dissolves}}}{Ca\,2\,HO}$ (a base)

Test for the base by litmus paper.

The last two reactions reveal the fact that there are different kinds of oxides.

The two principal classes of oxides are:—

1. **Acid-forming oxides.**
2. **Basic oxides.**

The first are oxides of negative elements and they unite *directly* with water to form acids, as in reaction (b) of EXP. 4.

The second are oxides of positive elements (metals) and unite directly with water to form bases, as in reaction of EXP. 5.

Acid-forming oxides are often called **anhydrides** (without water), since they may be considered as acids deprived of water.

EXAMPLE.

SO_2 = sulphuro*us* anhydride.

(The older chemists c lled the anhydride the acid, as SO_2 = sulphur-*ous* acid, but this is not now correct usage.)

Basic oxides are often called **bases.** (It is important to know that this is still correct usage. Indeed, some authors give as the definition, "A base is a metallic oxide," and these authors call the true base a "hydrated oxide" or "hydrated base.") Basic oxides unite with acids to form salts, just as the true bases do, and by a reaction very similar.

It will be seen that the term "base" is used by chemists somewhat indefinitely. In a wide sense it is used of any substance that will unite with an acid to form a salt (or a salt and water, or a salt with *free* hydrogen, etc.). In this wide sense it would include:—

1. Positive elements (or groupings).
2. Basic oxides.
3. Positive hydrates.

The word "base" has thus far been used in this last and restricted sense. The word "alkali" is also used in a comprehensive sense. The sense of the words, however, may easily be told from the connection.

CHAPTER XV.

Class 2.

Reaction by Change of Partners.

Exp. 6.—Dissolve one gram of sodium chloride (common salt) in nine grams of (distilled) water (a ten per cent. solution). Dissolve one gram of silver nitrate (lunar caustic) in nineteen grams of water (a five per cent. solution). Pour a little of the first solution into a small test-tube, and into it let fall a few drops taken from the second, by means of a glass tube pipette dipped beneath the solution and closed at the opposite end by the finger. A beautiful, white, curdy solid (silver chloride) is formed by the reaction, and slowly settles to the bottom of the test-tube.

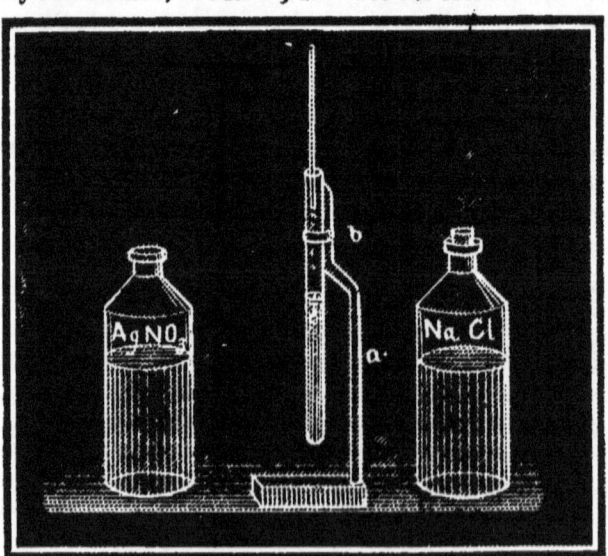

Fig. 4. (a)—lead post. (b)—rubber band.

Taking this reaction as the type of its class, we may learn much from it.

REACTIONS.

Just as by change of partners,

$$\{ \text{George} \atop \text{Lucy} \} + \{ \text{Charles} \atop \text{Emma} \} \stackrel{\text{become}}{=} \{ \text{George} \atop \text{Emma} \} + \{ \text{Charles} \atop \text{Lucy} \}$$

so

$$\underset{\substack{\text{sodium}\\ \text{chloride}}}{\text{Na Cl}} + \underset{\substack{\text{silver}\\ \text{nitrate}}}{\text{Ag NO}_3} = \underset{\substack{\text{sodium}\\ \text{nitrate}\\ \text{\{Soluble solid and therefore not precipitated, but remaining in solution.\}}}}{\text{Na NO}_3} + \underset{\substack{\text{silver}\\ \text{chloride}\\ \text{\{Insoluble solid, called a precipitate.\}}}}{\text{Ag Cl}}$$

NOTE.—This is a very simple and frequent method of reaction. Filter, wash, and preserve all precipitates for future use in experiments, or as samples of the various compounds. (See EXP. 7.) Carefully label the vials in which precipitates are preserved. It will be noticed that Ag Cl *turns dark* when exposed to the light. (See SILVER.)

Water favors chemical change.

(There are exceptions.—Water does not favor ordinary combustion.) Thus, two substances in solution will react with each other, which would not if they were mixed dry. Iron rusts (unites slowly with the oxygen of the air, forming ferric oxide Fe_2O_3) if exposed to the air wet. Knives and forks must be wiped dry, else they rust. **Solution** divides a substance more minutely and evenly than can be done by any other method of mechanical division. Solution separates the molecules. For instance, if a teaspoonful of common salt be thrown into a barrel of water and dissolved, molecules of salt may be found in every drop of the entire barrel. They seem to move among the molecules of water freely, the water giving them an atmosphere in which they easily perform reactions with other substances. The water is not written in the reaction, unless it really takes some part in the atomic changes.

When a substance dissolves in water, and unites chemically with the water to form another compound (as in reactions of EXP. 4 and 5), this is not a mere solution, but something more. In a *mere* solution the substance goes into the water (somewhat as grains of sand might be poured into a measure of peas) without uniting with the molecules of water at all.

A gas, as we have already learned, may be dissolved in water as well as a solid.

A liquid may also be dissolved in water, but we speak of the liquid not as dissolved in water, but as *diluted with water* (or mixed) and we do not speak of the resulting liquid as a solution. (See VOLATILE OILS.)

When as much as possible of the substance is dissolved in a certain amount of water, the solution is said to be a **saturated solution.**

Many solids and gases are insoluble in water. (Some liquids will not mix with water and therefore cannot be diluted with water.) Often these may be dissolved in other liquids, as alcohol (ethyl hydrate), hydrochloric acid, etc. The liquid dissolving the substance is called a **solvent.**

Whenever two substances, one at least being in solution, react, forming a solid insoluble in the liquid, the resulting solid, as it usually quickly falls to the bottom, is appropriately called a **precipitate.** If soluble solids are formed at the same time, they of course remain in solution. If gases are formed in the reaction, they come off from the liquids in bubbles. Substances which react with each other as in the above reaction, especially those that are much used in the chemical laboratory, are called **reagents.**

EXP. 7.—Into a test-tube containing silver nitrate solution let fall a few drops of dilute hydrochloric acid. The chemicals react by change of partners, as in EXP. 6, thus:—

Reaction: $\underset{\text{hydrogen chloride}}{HCl} + \underset{\text{silver nitrate}}{Ag\,NO_3} = \underset{\text{hydrogen nitrate}}{H\,NO_3} + \underset{\substack{\text{silver chloride} \\ \text{(precipitate)}}}{Ag\,Cl}$

Precipitates may be separated from the liquid by **filtration.** Cut and fold some filter paper, thus:—

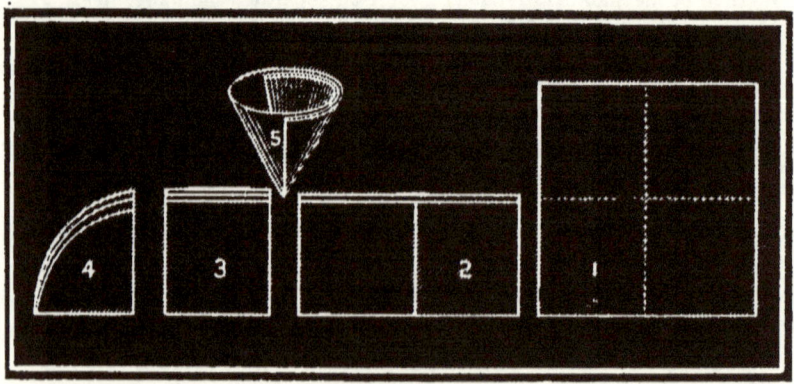

Fig. 5.

and place it on a funnel (tunnel), pouring the contents of the test-tube upon it.

REACTIONS.

Fig. 6.—Section of Filter Stand.

The precipitate remains upon the filter, while the liquid called **filtrate** passes through. Wash the precipitate, to free it entirely from the filtrate, by forcing with the breath water in fine spray from wash bottles upon it. Remove the precipitate and dry upon glass, or dry before removing, as is sometimes more convenient.

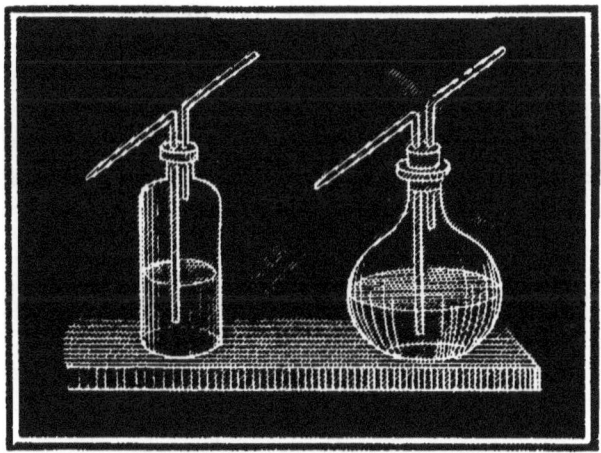

Fig. 7.
Bottle for cold water.   Flask for hot water.

CHAPTER XVI.

CLASS 2.—(continued.)

EXP. 8.—Place a very little ferrous sulphide in a small bottle, and pour upon it dilute sulphuric acid. [In some cases the reaction is n t prompt. This depends upon preparation of Fe S used. Heat acid and Fe S in test-tube, Fig. 3 and Fig. 18.]

Reaction: Fe S $+$ H$_2$SO$_4$ $=$ Fe SO$_4$ $+$ H$_2$S

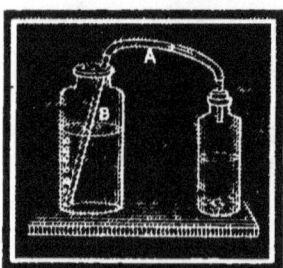

Fig. 8.—Making solution of hydrogen sulphide.

As H$_2$S is a gas, it comes off in bubbles. Close the mouth of the flask by a rubber cork, through which a fine glass tube passes. By means of a rubber tube and another glass tube, allow the gas to pass into water. As the gas is soluble (*three* volumes in one of water), we have a solution of the gas. Set this aside carefully corked, as a *reagent*. (It decomposes in about four weeks and becomes worthless.)

Caution.—H$_2$S is a poisonous gas, and EXP. 8 should be performed under a gas chimney, or near a window with an *outward* draft. (To breathe a *small* quantity mixed with air will, however, do no harm.) This gas is largely used in the laboratory, and chemists are often more careless with it than is consistent with health. Learn to be *cautious* and *careful* in performing all experiments, *following directions minutely.*

EXP. 9.—To a solution of lead acetate in test-tube add drop by drop solution of H$_2$S. (Reagents are hereafter presumed to be in solution.)

Reaction: Pb 2 C$_2$H$_3$O$_2$ $+$ H$_2$S $=$ Pb S $+$ 2 H C$_2$H$_3$O$_2$
lead   hydrogen   lead   hydrogen
acetate   sulphide   sulphide   acetate
(black precipitate)

It will be noticed that when the hydrogen changes partners with the lead atom and takes the acetate grouping, the hydrogen and acetate grouping being univalent, they are matched *one* to *one*, giving us two

REACTIONS. 41

molecules of acetic acid. It would be incorrect to write $H_2\ 2\ C_2H_3O_2$. Never put *two* monads with *two* monads in reactions, but always *one* monad with *one* monad, and if there be two of each, double the molecule.

Just as we must take *two* monads to match *one* dyad in a binary, so we must take *two* molecules containing monad partners to react with *one* molecule containing dyad partners.

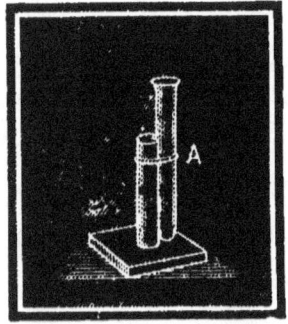

Fig. 9.—(A) rubber band.

Exp. 10.—To mercuric chloride (corrosive sublimate) add drop by drop potassium iodide. (Fig. 9 represents a convenient test-tube stand.)

Reaction: $\underset{\text{mercuric chloride}}{HgCl_2} + \underset{\text{potassium iodide}}{2KI} =$

$\underset{\substack{\text{mercuric iodide}\\\text{(red precipitate)}}}{HgI_2} + \underset{\text{potassium chloride}}{2KCl}$

If too little is added, the precipitate dissolves; if too much is added, the precipitate dissolves, *i. e.*, the precipitate dissolves in excess of either reagent. Notice that the molecule of mercuric chloride contains *dyad* partners (Hg = a dyad, and Cl_2 two monads = a dyad,) while potassium iodide contains *monad* partners; therefore, we must take *two* molecules of the latter to react with *one* of the former.

Exp. 11.—Into a solution of arsenous oxide (dissolve in hot water and filter) let fall a few drops of dilute hydrochloric acid.

Reaction (a): $As_2O_3 + 6HCl = 2AsCl_3 + 3H_2O$

As_2O_3, a molecule containing hexad partners, requires *six* molecules of H Cl to react with it. As Cl_3, arsenous chloride, being soluble in water, does not appear as a precipitate. Into the test-tube drop solution of H_2S.

Reaction (b): $2AsCl_3 + 3H_2S = \underset{\substack{\text{(lemon yellow}\\\text{precipitate)}}}{As_2S_3} + 6HCl$

In reaction (b) we must take *two* molecules containing triad partners (As Cl_3) to react with *three* molecules containing dyad partners (H_2S), just as we take *two* triad elements to match *three* dyad elements in forming binaries. In the second member of the equation we must be careful to match the atoms according to their "strength" and to multiply the molecules *afterward*, so that the number of atoms of any element shall be the same in both members.

Exp. 12.—To lead acetate (sugar of lead) add magnesium sulphate.

Reaction: $Pb\ 2C_2H_3O_2$ + $Mg\ SO_4$ = $Pb\ SO_4$ + $Mg\ 2C_2H_3O_2$
        a poison   its antidote   insoluble and   soluble, but harm-
                                   therefore harmless   less salt
                                  (white precipitate)

Inspection of this last reaction will reveal the exact nature of a *chemical* antidote. Let the test-tube represent the stomach. **A chemical antidote** is a substance which will unite with the poison, forming insoluble or harmless compounds, or both. (See ANTIDOTES.)

Exp. 13.—To calcium hydrate (lime water) add ammonium carbonate.

Reaction: $Ca\ 2\ HO + (H_4N)_2\ CO_3 = Ca\ CO_3 + 2\ H_4N\ HO$
                                                white precipitate
                                                  (chalk)

Inspection of the following questions and the method of solving them will open to the attentive student a wide field for careful and accurate work. To such a student the problems are not difficult.

1. From 542 mgs. of mercuric chloride, how much mercuric iodide could be made by adding potassium iodide?

Reaction: $Hg\ Cl_2 + 2\ K\ I = Hg\ I_2 + 2\ K\ Cl$
                 200   200
                  71   254
               271 mol. wt.   454 mol. wt.

                       (will make)
271 mgs. $Hg\ Cl_2$ = 454 mgs. $Hg\ I_2$
1   "   "   = $\frac{1}{271}$ of 454 $Hg\ I_2$
542 "   "   = $\frac{542}{271}$ of 454 mgs. $Hg\ I_2$ = 908 mgs.—*Ans.*

2. How much mercuric chloride will be required to make 150 gms. of mercuric iodide (adding K I)?

Reaction: $HgCl_2 + 2KI = HgI_2 + 2KCl$

```
             200              200
              71              254
             ---              ---
             271              454
```

454 Hg I$_2$ = 271 Hg Cl$_2$ *(would require)*

1 " = $\frac{1}{454}$ of 271 Hg Cl$_2$

150 gms. " = $\frac{150}{454}$ of 271 gms. Hg Cl$_2$ = $89\frac{122}{227}$ gms.—*Ans.*

3. How much potassium iodide would be required to make 227 gms. of Hg I$_2$? *Ans.* 166 gms.

4. How much potassium chloride could be made by using 996 gms. of potassium iodide? *Ans.* 447 gms.

CHAPTER XVII.

CLASS 3.

Reaction of **Acid** and **Base**.

When an *acid* and *base* are united, the result is a **salt** and **water.** The acid is said to *neutralize* the base (or *vice versa*).

EXP. 14.—To barium hydrate add drop by drop sulphuric acid.

Reaction: Ba 2 HO + H$_2$SO$_4$ = Ba SO$_4$ + 2 H$_2$O
 base   acid   salt   water
                    (white precipitate)

EXP. 15.—To oxalic acid add calcium hydrate.

Reaction: H$_2$C$_2$O$_4$ + Ca 2 HO = Ca C$_2$O$_4$ + 2 H$_2$O
 acid   base   salt   water
                    (white precipitate)

EXP. 16.—To sodium hydrate add drop by drop acetic acid, till solution is neutral to litmus paper.

Reaction: Na HO + H C$_2$H$_3$O$_2$ = Na C$_2$H$_3$O$_2$ + H$_2$O
 base   acid   salt   water

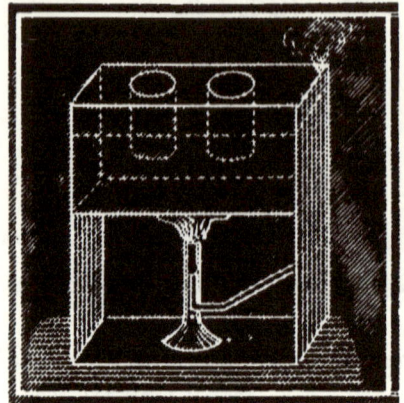

Fig. 10.—Water Bath.

There is no precipitate, because sodium acetate is soluble in water.

Filter to remove any slight solid impurities and evaporate to dryness in evaporating dish (or beaker) over a **water bath,** *i. e.*, steam bath. (See Fig. 10.) Sodium acetate, a solid, remains.

Note. — Whenever a water bath is recommended, the simple meaning is that the evaporation be carefully done, so as not to scorch or sublime the residue.

The water bath prevents the heat from rising above 100° C. It may be dispensed with in most cases if sufficient care be used.

Class 3 is only another form of Class 2. In reactions of Class 3 the same law holds good, viz.: "That *two* molecules containing *monad* partners must be taken to react with *one* molecule containing *dyad* partners, etc."

Class 4.

Reactions of **Acids** and **Carbonates.**

In these reactions, the carbonate grouping breaks up. When an *acid* unites with a *carbonate*, the result is a **salt, water,** and **carbonic oxide** (a gas). The law in regard to molecules containing partners of different strengths holds good, as in the last two cases. This reaction is frequently used by the druggist and pharmacist.

Exp. 17.—To acetic acid add sodium carbonate (solid or in solution) till effervescence ceases. (**Effervescence** is the bubbling caused by the rapid separation of a gas from a liquid.)

Reaction: $\underset{\text{carbonate}}{Na_2CO_3} + \underset{\text{acid}}{2\ H\ C_2H_3O_2} = \underset{\substack{\text{salt}\\ \text{(soluble)}}}{2\ Na\ C_2H_3O_2} + \underset{\text{water}}{H_2O} + \underset{\substack{\text{carbonic}\\ \text{oxide}}}{C\ O_2}$

Filter, evaporate filtrate, and preserve. The salt is obtained as in Exp. 16. The heat of evaporation entirely expels any CO_2 that may be held in solution after the reaction.

REACTIONS. 45

Exp. 18. —Into dilute citric acid let fall an *excess* of finely pulverized calcium carbonate (marble). When effervescence ceases, *boil* (to precipitate any dissolved carbonate), filter, evaporate, and preserve as before.

Reaction: $\underset{\text{carbonate}}{3 \text{ Ca CO}_3} + \underset{\text{acid}}{2 \text{ H}_3\text{C}_6\text{H}_5\text{O}_7} = \underset{\text{salt}}{\text{Ca}_3\, 2\, \text{C}_6\text{H}_5\text{O}_7} + \underset{\text{water}}{3 \text{ H}_2\text{O}} + \underset{\substack{\text{carbonic}\\ \text{oxide}}}{3 \text{ CO}_2}$

NOTE.—*Three* molecules containing *dyad* partners ($Ca''CO_3''$) must react with *two* molecules containing *triad* partners ($H_3'''C_6H_5O_7'''$), as before. (See also Exp. 33.)

Notice, in evaporating, that this salt (calcium citrate) is less soluble in *hot* than in *cold* water; an exception to the general rule, that "for equal volumes, *hot water dissolves more of a solid than cold water.*

As a rule, "*hot water dissolves less of a gas* than an equal volume of cold water." Indeed, many gases not only will not dissolve at all in boiling water, but may be completely expelled from water, in which they may have been previously dissolved, by boiling it.

Before leaving these chapters on reactions, the student should be able to write promptly any reaction belonging to either of the four classes, provided he has the *names* of the two substances given *and the two reference tables before him.*

MISCELLANEOUS PROBLEMS.

1. Write formulas for five binary acids.
2. Write formulas for ten ternary salts.
3. Write formulas for two binary salts.
4. Write formulas for six ternary acids.
5. Write formulas for five bases.
6. In 150 gms. of arsenous oxide, how much As?
7. In 1000 gms. of silver chloride, how much silver?
8. How much mercuric sulphide could be made by using 50 kgs. of mercury (Hg'')?
9. Reaction when phosphorus burns in air?
10. When carbon burns?

Reactions when the following are united:—

11. Stannous chloride (Sn'') and hydrogen sulphide?
12. Copper sulphate and sodium hydrate?

13. Sodium carbonate and hydrochloric acid?
14. Ammonium carbonate and calcium hydrate?
15. Potassium hydrate and sulphuric acid?
16. Calcium hydrate and citric acid?
17. Potassium *carbonate* and tartaric acid?
18. Acetic acid and magnesium *carbonate?*
19. To make 190 gms. of magnesium chloride (by adding H Cl), how much magnesium *carbonate* must be taken?
20. How much arsenous oxide, As_2O_3 (white arsenic) was contained in a vessel full of water, from which 15 mgs. of arsenous sulphide was precipitated (by adding H Cl and H_2S)?

CHAPTER XVIII.

OXYGEN.

EXP. 19.—Carefully pulverize in a mortar a small quantity of potassium chlorate, and, having mixed it thoroughly with an equal bulk of *pure* manganese dioxide, introduce into a small copper retort. Heat by a strong alcohol flame, or flame from a Bunsen's burner. Collect O in receivers over a pneumatic tub, as represented in Fig. 11. [A glass flask *heated upon a sand bath* (iron basin filled with sand, Fig. 21) may be used in place of the copper retort.]

Reaction: $K Cl O_3 = K Cl + O_3$

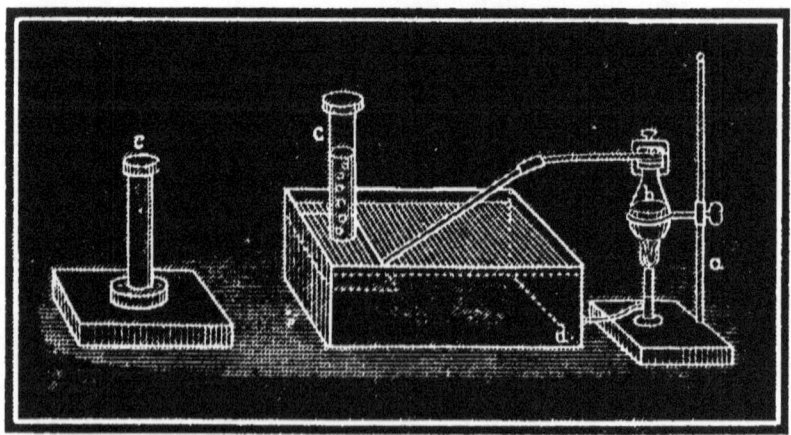

Fig. 11
(a)—retort stand; (b)—retort; (c)—receiver; (d)—pneumatic tub; (e,—receiver removed.

OXYGEN. 47

NOTE.—The presence of Mn O$_2$ causes the O to come off more steadily and at a lower temperature, but as it takes no part in the reaction, (?) it is not written. The first bubbles that come off are composed principally of air from the retort and should be allowed to escape. The O often looks *cloudy*, because small particles of the salt and oxide are carried over by the *draft*. These gradually dissolve or settle into the water. Three or four receivers should be inverted, and as fast as filled removed by means of a small, shoal tin cover, holding a little water, to prevent the escape of the gas. Small quantities of O may be conveniently made by using test-tubes as retorts, test-tubes, or bottles, as receivers, and a beaker or basin as a pneumatic tub. (See Fig. 3.) Avoid heating too rapidly in one place, by carrying lamp or burner back and forth slowly, so that test-tube shall pass through the bottom of the flame, nearly touching the wick or burner.

Caution.—K Cl O$_3$ must not be heated alone. Commercial Mn O$_2$ is sometimes adulterated with carbon (pounded coal) and when mixed with K.Cl O$_3$ and heated, the mixture explodes violently. Test by heating in test-tube a small quantity of the oxide and chlorate mixed, unless the former is warranted to be pure. The delivery tube must be removed from the water *before* the heat is taken from the retort, otherwise, as the gas in the retort cools and contracts, the water is forced back along the tube by atmospheric pressure. The first that falls into the highly heated retort is instantly converted into steam, causing an explosion. Ordinary care will prevent any serious accident. The chief danger in breaking glass retorts is to the eyes.

Learn here that an explosion is (generally) caused by the *sudden* conversion of matter from the *solid* or *liquid* to the *gaseous* state.

Oxygen is a colorless **gas,** without odor or taste. As we have inferred from the formulas thus far used, it is a *very* **abundant element.** It exists **free** (uncombined) **in the air,** forming one-fifth its volume. Chemically combined with other elements, it forms by weight eight-ninths of water, one-half of minerals, three-fourths of animal tissues, and four-fifths of vegetable tissues; in short, so far as we know, about two-thirds of the earth.

EXP. 20.—Into a receiver (bottle) of O, plunge a taper having a live coal upon the end, it immediately bursts into a blaze. Quickly remove and blow out the flame. Repeat the relighting from twenty to forty times, as may easily be done before the gas is exhausted. Do not plunge deeper than is necessary to rekindle, as this uses up the O rapidly.

Wood, oil, tallow, etc. (things that we ordinarily burn), are composed principally of H and C, and are therefore called **hydrocarbons**. When hydrocarbons (as the taper in the experiment) burn, two reactions take place, viz.:—

$$H_2 + O = H_2O \text{ (steam)}$$
$$C + O_2 = CO_2 \text{ (a gas)}$$
Gaseous products of the combustion.

Immediately after the O is exhausted, pour into the receiver a very small quantity of water, and closing its mouth, shake at intervals. The CO_2 gradually dissolves.

Reaction: $CO_2 + H_2O = H_2CO_3$
acid forming oxide — acid

Test by litmus paper, but as H_2CO_3 is a very weak acid, litmus paper must remain a little time in it.

O is a **vigorous supporter of combustion.** O is *heavier than air*, for we hold the mouth of the receiver upward to retain the gas.

Water is the standard of specific gravity for solids and liquids, and air for gases (in physics). Sp. gr. of air is 1, of O 1.1+. But in chemistry, **hydrogen** (which see) is made the standard for gases.

Fig. 12.

EXP. 21.—Straighten a narrow steel(Fe)watch-spring and file the end bright. Attach (Fig. 12) a very short piece (head) of a common match, as kindling for the steel. Ignite by flame and quickly plunge into a receiver of O. The steel burns vividly

Reaction: $Fe_3 + O_4 = Fe_3O_4$
(triferric tetroxide black or magnetic iron oxide)

If a large receiver is used, and the head of the match is attached to the spring by winding a very fine iron wire closely about both, the experiment is a very brilliant one. As this oxide of iron does not unite with water, the water shaken up in the receiver has no effect upon litmus paper. Though a positive oxide, it is not a basic oxide. This reaction is an irregular one, that is, the strength of iron is apparently not according to the Table.

OXYGEN.

If the air were pure O undiluted with N, our iron stoves would take fire, and a general conflagration would spread over the earth. We could not, for any length of time, breathe pure O, as it would so stimulate the vital processes as to produce speedy death. A small animal placed in a jar of constantly renewed O, dies in a few hours.

Exp. 22.—Charcoal *bark*, a small part of which has been heated to a live coal, plunged into O (by means of a Cu wire twisted about it), bursts into a vivid combustion.

Exp. 23.—Repeat Exp. 4 in jar of O. (Place S on chalk in a combustion spoon. Copper wire twisted about a piece of chalk makes a good combustion spoon.)

Exp. 24.—Cut under water, quickly and carefully dry between pieces of blotting-paper, a small piece of phosphorus (not larger than a grain of wheat). Place in a combustion spoon, ignite by hot wire, while lowering into a large jar of O, containing at the bottom a little water. A blinding light is caused by the combustion.

Reaction: $P_4 + O_5 = P_2O_5$
dense white fumes

Fig. 13.

In a short time these fumes are dissolved in the water, and the following reaction slowly takes place:—

$$P_2O_5 + 3 H_2O = 2 H_3PO_4$$
acid forming oxide

Test by litmus paper.

Caution.—Handle P with great care, on no account touching it. The heat of the hand may inflame it, and its burns are dangerous. Its vapor is highly poisonous and must not be inhaled. The dense, white fumes should be immediately shut in by stopple attached to combustion spoon. (See Fig. 13.)

O is an exceedingly **active** gas. It alone supports all ordinary burning that takes place in the air. *To bring this gas in contact with the blood* is the object of respiration in animals. The blood absorbs and carries O to all the tissues, the most prominent chemical change taking place in the body being that of *oxidation*. (See carbonic oxide.)

There is a peculiar form of condensed O, called **Ozone**. It is O in an *allotropic* state. It may be made in various ways, especially by the action of electricity on common O. It occurs in minute quantities in the air. It is even more active than O and is a powerful **disinfectant**.

In ozone tainted meat rapidly loses its putrescent odor, because the foul material is oxidized, forming *relatively* wholesome compounds. The molecule of *ozone* may be represented thus [O / OO] with *three* atoms, that of oxygen being OO composed of *two* atoms, that is, three volumes of oxygen if it could all be changed to ozone would make but two volumes of ozone.

CHAPTER XIX.

HYDROGEN.

EXP. 25.—Place in a small flask, or large test-tube (hydrogen generator), some granulated Zn. Upon it pour dilute (10 per cent.) sulphuric acid. Close mouth of flask with perforated rubber cork, through which passes a fine glass tube. Collect H over pneumatic tub, as in Fig. 14.

$$Zn + H_2SO_4 = ZnSO_4 + H_2$$

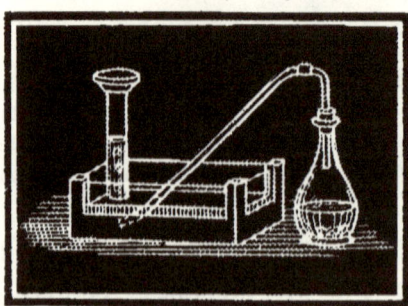

Fig. 14.—Making Hydrogen.

NOTE.—Collect several receivers of the gas, and, after the reaction has ceased, filter the liquid remaining in the flask; evaporate filtrate, and the white salt, zinc sulphate, is obtained. If a drop of the filtrate is placed on a piece of glass and set aside, *away from the dust*, beautiful crystals of the salt are left upon the glass.

HYDROGEN. 51

Hydrogen is a colorless gas, without odor or taste (when *pure*). It is the essential constituent, as we have seen, **in acids.** Indeed, acids have sometimes been defined as "salts of hydrogen." H does not occur *free*. It has been condensed by cold and pressure, first, to a liquid and then to a white solid. H is not poisonous, but destroys life, just as water does, by shutting out the O. The lungs may be inflated with the *pure* gas without harm.

Caution.—Gases made by beginners must never be breathed. As a rule, a gas is obtained absolutely *pure* with great difficulty. For methods of obtaining gases pure, see larger text-books or some treatise.

EXP. 26.—Remove a jar of H, holding the mouth downward, and into it plunge slender lighted taper. The H takes fire and burns at the mouth of jar, but the taper is extinguished in the gas above. It may be relighted by the burning H as it is being removed.

H is **lighter than air,** for we hold the gas by keeping the mouth of the receiver downward. H is **very inflammable,** *i. e.*, its igniting point is low. It **does not support combustion** (of hydrocarbons).

NOTE.—Combustible bodies and supporters of combustion are relative terms. A jet of O would burn in a jar of H just as well as a jet of H in a jar of O. One as well as the other could be called the supporter of the combustion.

EXP. 27.— Collect H from generator in test-tube by **displacement** of air. Pour upward into another test-tube, displacing the air. Test by igniting.

EXP. 28.—Attach by rubber tube a clay pipe to generator and blow soap bubbles with H. They ascend and may be ignited in the air.

Hydrogen is the **lightest substance known,** being about $14\frac{1}{2}$ times lighter than air. Chemists take hydrogen as the standard of specific gravity for gases. With this standard, *"one-half its molecular weight is the specific gravity of any gas."* (See Miscellaneous Questions, Chap. XXII, NOTE.)

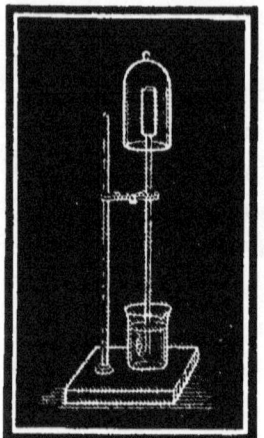

Fig. 15.

EXP. 29.—Fit a perforated cork, through which passes a glass tube, deeply into a *new, dry* porous cup (such as is used in Bunsen's battery). Melt over the surface of the cork sufficient paraffine (or tallow) to make it airtight. Place the end of tube just beneath water in a beaker (Fig. 15), and cover the porous cup with receiver of H. The H passes by diffusion in through the pores of the cup much more rapidly than the air passes out, therefore bubbles of air are forced out through the water. Remove receiver and soon the water rises in the tube because of the diffusion of the H outward.

All gases possess power of **diffusion**, but the power is possessed by H in an extreme degree. The diffusibility of gases is *"inversely as the square roots of their densities,"* the density (or sp. gr.) of any gas being, as given above, half its molecular weight.

EXAMPLE.

$$\sqrt{\tfrac{16}{\text{density of O}}} \; : \; \sqrt{\tfrac{1}{\text{density of H}}} \; : : \; \underset{\text{of H}}{4\ \text{diffusibility}} \; : \; \underset{\text{of O}}{1\ \text{diffusibility}}$$

That is, H has four times the diffusive power of O, or diffuses four times as rapidly. H may leak through vessels that would retain O permanently.

Fig. 16.—Philosopher's lamp.

EXP. 30.—Close generating flask by a rubber stopple, through which passes a *hard* glass tube, with fine opening. *After the air has been expelled by the* H, ignite the jet. The apparatus is the "Philosopher's Lamp." Over the flame invert a cold, dry test-tube. It is bedewed with moisture.

$$H_2 + O = H_2O$$

When H burns, the **product** is water (steam). The H flame gives **little light,** but **great heat.** The alcohol (ethyl hydrate) flame gives little light and great heat, because alcohol contains much H.

The flame of the **oxy-hydrogen blowpipe** melts many substances (as platinum), infusible in ordinary fire, the alcohol flame, or the flame from a Bunsen's burner.

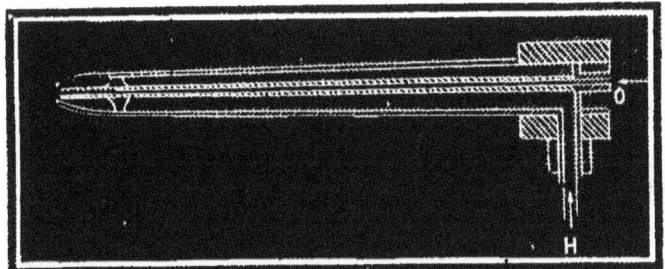

Fig. 17.—Section of oxy-hydrogen blowpipe.

The H from the gasholder is first turned on and ignited, and afterward the O is turned on.

Exp. 31.—Fill over a pneumatic tub a stout quart fruit jar one-third with O, and the remainder with H. *Wrap about it a cloth;* remove, and, holding the mouth downward, quickly ignite by means of a taper. A sharp explosion ensues.

There are two reports heard as one, the second so closely follows the first. The first is caused by the sudden (but not greater than a few volumes) expansion of the gases heated by their union; the second is caused by (the steam suddenly condensing) the rush of the air from all sides to fill the partial vacuum. **Caution.**—Of course, H explodes when mixed with air. Care must be taken to expel all air from apparatus before igniting jets of H. Never ignite large quantities of the gas.

Exp. 32.—Repeat the experiment of decomposing water as explained in connection with Fig. 1.

This proves by **Analysis** the composition of water. If we explode *two* volumes of H with *one* of O and find we have nothing but water left, we prove the composition of water by **Synthesis.**

$$\text{Water } H_2O$$

The wonderful power of **chemical affinity** is shown in

this compound. A union of the most inflammable substance known with the most vigorous supporter of combustion, forms another substance which will extinguish fires. We have called this substance by its pet name, because it is so common a substance and so generally distributed. Its systematic name (hydrogen oxide) is seldom used. We have already learned that **water** is the general **solvent** in nature, dissolving most gases and solids and diluting most liquids.

Hard water contains minerals in solution; soft water does not.

NOTE.—In a narrower, but very common usage, only such water is called *hard* as contains in solution minerals *that either react with soap*, or hinder its solution (see SOAP). Water containing such minerals as borax and potassium carbonate would be called in the laundry soft water. Water or soil containing potassium carbonate, sodium carbonate, etc., is often said to be "*alkaline*," because these salts have an alkaline reaction upon litmus, and because the old chemists called the strongly positive carbonates "mild alkalies." (They called the strongly positive hydrates "caustic alkalies," and these hydrates are still frequently thus called.)

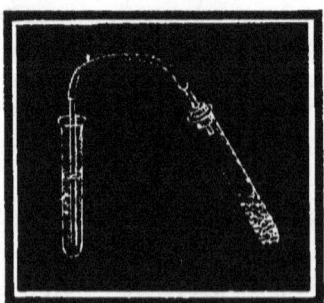

Fig. 18.

EXP. 33.—In a test-tube place small pieces of marble and cover with dilute hydrochloric acid (ten per cent).

Reaction (Class 4th):—

$Ca CO_3 + 2 H Cl = C . Cl_2 + H_2O + CO_2$

By means of a delivery tube (Fig. 18) pass the gas through clear lime water (solution of Ca 2 HO, see EXP. 5) in a second test-tube. The lime water at first becomes milky because of white precipitate of Ca CO_3.

Reaction: $Ca\ 2\ HO\ +\ CO_2\ =\ Ca CO_3\ +\ H_2O$
                   base   acl forming   salt
                              oxide

Allow the gas to continue bubbling through the lime water. After all the Ca is thrown down as a carbonate, the CO_2 dissolves in the water. *Carbonates dissolve in water containing CO_2 in solution, but not in pure water.)* The water becomes clear again because the calcium carbonate is dissolved. This clear water is now water of "temporary hardness." Boil. The CO_2 in *solution* is driven off, and the calcium carbonate is again precipitated, being insoluble in pure water.

Hardness produced by earthy (**Ca. Mg.** Sr. Ba., etc.) carbonates is called "**temporary hardness,**" because the carbonate may be precipitated by boiling, leaving the water soft. The "fur" upon the tea-kettle is a precipitated carbonate.

Hardness produced by earthy sulphates is called "**permanent hardness,**" because the water cannot be made soft by boiling. (See SOAP.)

The vapor of water in the atmosphere is essential, not only to plant life, but to animal life as well. The earth would be a vast desert were it not that tons of water are constantly being carried up from the ocean by **evaporation,** so that the air currents may distribute it, not alone to fall as rain, but also to keep the atmosphere everywhere moist.

Many substances, when they crystallize (assume a symmetrical shape in solidifying), take up a definite amount of water, called **water of crystallization.** This may be expelled by heat, but the *essential* properties of the substance are not changed.

EXP. 34.—Heat in a narrow, deep test-tube of hard glass, small crystals of pure copper sulphate previously carefully weighed; the **water of crystallization** is expelled and part of it condenses in small drops on the cooler part of the test-tube. The blue color disappears. Wipe with dry cloth the water from the test-tube. Remove and weigh the sulphate. It has lost over one-third its weight, as the formula of *crystallized* copper sulphate is $Cu\,S\,O_4, 5\,H_2O$. Touch with a drop of water, the color slowly returns. Dissolve in a small quantity of water, evaporate slightly, and set aside to cool. Beautiful **crystals** of copper sulphate form as the solution cools.

Fine **crystals** of various substances may be formed in this way, viz., by making saturated solution of the substance (slightly evaporating), and setting aside for a few days. Making a collection of crystals will be found a very profitable exercise.

Water of crystallization is not written in ordinary reactions of substances in solution, but must be taken into account in dealing with the dry solids. Of course a larger quantity of the crystallized solid must be taken to equal a smaller quantity of the uncrystallized, *if the solid takes up water of crystallization.*

Some substances, such as sodium acetate (Na $C_2H_3O_2$ 3 H_2O), sodium carbonate ($Na_2 C O_3$, 10 H_2O), etc., when exposed to the air lose their water of crystallization, and crumble to powder. These are said to be **efflorescent.**

Some substances, as potassium carbonate ($K_2 C O_3$), when exposed to the air, absorb moisture and dissolve (or partially dissolve). These are said to be **deliquescent.**

The law of physics, that "heat expands and cold contracts," does not hold with water in cooling from about 4° (C) to 0°, through which space it steadily expands, until it freezes (crystallizes) at 0°. At the moment of freezing there is a sudden and great expansion. (See Plot b, Fig. 19.) The importance of this exception cannot be overestimated, for it makes *ice lighter than water*, and so prevents lakes and rivers from freezing solid.

Water containing impurities in solution may be purified by **distillation.** The water is placed in a **retort,** or "**still,**" is heated, rises as steam (at 100°), which, passing through the **condenser** (supplied with cold water in direction of arrows, Fig. 19), condenses, and is collected in a receiver. Steam ("**dry steam**") is an invisible gas. That which is seen and often miscalled steam is steam condensed (or partially condensed) into minute globules of water and held in suspension (like dust) by the air or by the invisible steam, in which case the steam is called **"wet steam."**)

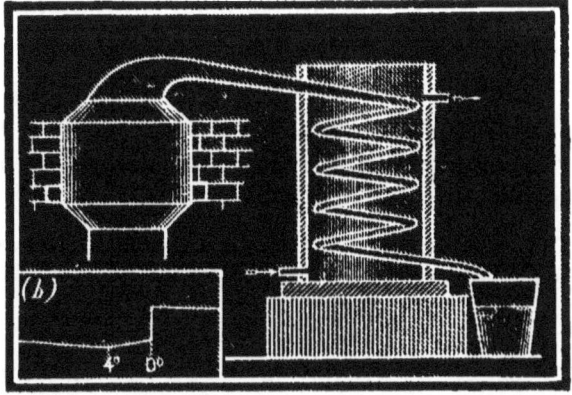

Fig. 19.—Retort, or "still," and condenser. Plot b—Effect of "cold" upon water.

CHAPTER XX.

NITROGEN.

EXP. 35.—Place a piece of chalk on a tripod wire-holder, standing in a deep plate of water. Upon the chalk place a small piece of P. Ignite by hot wire and quickly invert a receiver over it. (**Caution,** EXP. 24.)

$$P_2 + O_5 = \underset{\substack{\text{soluble}\\ \text{white}\\ \text{fumes}}}{P_2O_5}$$

Fig. 20.

The P unites with the O in the jar. The phosphoric oxide dissolves and the water rises by atmospheric pressure and fills one-fifth of the receiver, the space before occupied by the O. N remains in the receiver above the water, neither burning nor supporting the combustion of the remaining phosphorus. (See Phosphorus.)

Nitrogen is a colorless gas, without odor or taste. It forms by volume $\frac{4}{5}$ **of the atmosphere.** N is not poisonous, and destroys life only by shutting out O. It is **not inflammable** and it does **not support combustion.** It is a very **inert** element. It dilutes the active O of the air, and the mechanical mixture is thus fitted for respiration. Some of its *compounds* are by no means inert. For example, **"nitro-glycerine,"** the violent explosive, is **glyceryl nitrate,** and the deadly poison, prussic acid, is hydrogen cyanide. No one can predict with certainty the character of a chemical compound from the nature of its constituents.

It might be supposed that, N being lighter than O, the air would separate into two layers, the heavier, O, sinking. The two gases, however, are kept thoroughly mixed by the law of **diffusion of gases.**

N forms with O five oxides, viz.:—

N_2O, hyponitrous oxide (acid-forming).
N_2O_2 nitrogen dioxide.
N_2O_3 nitrous oxide (acid-forming).
N_2O_4 nitrogen tetroxide (or peroxide).
N_2O_5 nitric oxide (acid-forming).

These oxides illustrate well the great law of **multiple proportions.** When one substance unites *chemically* with another, it is in some definite proportion, *or* **multiple of that proportion.** Whenever substances are united *physically* (mechanically, as in alloys of metals, etc.) they may be united (mixed) in any proportion.

Note.—We see from the above that there is a third class of **indifferent oxides** (as N_2O_2, N_2O_4), neither acid-forming nor basic. The pupil need not give much attention, however, to this class. All the positive indifferent oxides, as MnO_2, BaO_2, K_2O_4, PbO_2, having more O than the basic, are called **peroxides.** For preparation of N_2O_3 and N_2O_5 see larger text-books.

NITROGEN. 59

EXP. 36.—Heat in flask ammonium nitrate and collect gas over pneumatic tub of *warm* water.

$$H_4N\ NO_3 = 2\ H_2O + N_2O$$

Hyponitrous oxide ("nitrous oxide" "laughing gas"), inhaled with a small proportion of O, produces a peculiar intoxication, hence its name of "laughing gas." If the pure gas is inhaled, it soon produces insensibility. It is much used as an **anæsthetic** by dentists and by surgeons in minor operations. It is kept condensed in liquid state in iron cylinders. (*See Caution, under Hydrogen, Exp. 25.*)

EXP. 37.—To small pieces of copper add dilute (50 per cent.) nitric acid, red fumes appear in generator (see EXP. 38), but a colorless gas collects over the tub.

Reaction (irregular, don't attempt to remember it):—

$$Cu_3 + 8\ H\ N\ O_3 = 3\ Cu\ 2\ N\ O_3 + 4\ H_2O + \underset{\text{nitrogen dioxide}}{N_2O_2}$$

After the action has ceased, filter water in flask, evaporate, and obtain blue crystals of Cu 2 N O₃.

EXP. 38.—Admit to test-tube containing N₂O₂ a bubble of O (or air). Red fumes of N₂O₄ appear.

$$N_2O_2 + O_2 = \underset{\text{nitrogen tetroxide}}{N_2O_4}$$

These fumes are very soluble in water, and the water slowly rises to take the place of the dissolved gas. If air is admitted, of course the water will not entirely fill the test-tube, as the N will remain undissolved above the water.

EXP. 39.—Into a test-tube put a small quantity (4 gms.) of sodium nitrate (or K NO₃) and 2 gms. of sulphuric acid. Carefully heat. Collect nitric acid in a narrow, deep test-tube, well cooled by sinking to its mouth in cold water. [Sink test-tube by tying stone to the bottom. Don't breathe the fumes.]

$$2\ Na\ N\ O_3 + H_2S\ O_4 = Na_2S\ O_4 + 2\ H\ N\ O_3$$

Nitric acid (old name **aqua fortis**) is prepared by heating sulphuric acid with sodium nitrate (but see acid-salts). It is a colorless (if pure), fuming, corrosive liquid.

Exp. 40.—Place a quill in HNO_3 and heat. The quill turns yellow.

Exp. 41.—To dilute HNO_3 add a crystal of $FeSO_4$; then add a few drops of H_2SO_4. A brown compound ($FeSO_4, N_2O_2$) slowly forms about the crystal. This is a good test for HNO_3 and other nitrates.

Exp. 42.—Throw a small crystal of potassium nitrate upon a red-hot coal. The coal burns rapidly (almost explosively).

Nitric acid stains organic matter, as the skin, nails, etc., a **dingy yellow.** It is a powerful **oxidizing agent,** as are all the other nitrates.

Exp. 43.—Spread upon a piece of clean copper (also upon a piece of iron) a *thin* layer of paraffine. Write upon each, taking care not to scratch the metal. Upon the writing put nitric acid (50 per cent.). It etches the words by oxidizing the metals, dissolving and uniting with the metallic oxides.

Nitric acid is used in **etching** upon copper and iron (copperplate, swords, razors).

Exp. 44.—Into a test-tube containing nitric acid, drop a piece of gold-leaf and heat. It does not dissolve. Add a few drops of hydrochloric acid. The gold rapidly dissolves, forming $AuCl_3$ in solution.

Nitric acid (about 3 parts) and **hydrochloric acid** (5 parts) form **aqua regia,** the solvent of gold (and platinum).

Exp. 45.—Place in a flask a little ammonium chloride (sal ammoniac) with an equal weight of calcium oxide (quicklime), each finely pulverized. Add a little water and, quickly closing flask, heat upon sand bath. Dry gas by passing through bottle containing CaO. Collect by displacement of air in receiver. (See Fig. 21.) ["Drying tube" may be dispensed with and gas passed directly from flask into receiver. Don't breathe too much of the gas.]

$$2H_4NCl + CaO = CaCl_2 + H_2O + 2H_3N$$

NITROGEN.

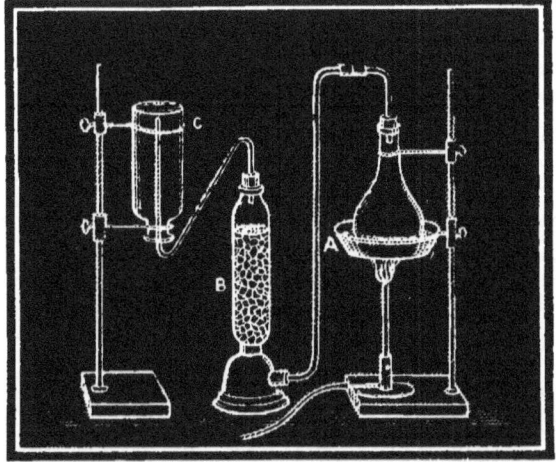

Fig. 21.—A—sand bath; B—drying tube; C receiver.

EXP. 46 (45 concluded).—Quickly close mouth of bottle of ammonia by perforated rubber cork, through which passes a glass tube drawn to a fine point and connected with water colored *red* by slightly acidulated litmus solution. Hasten the action by forcing air into lower flask (through tube A B, Fig. 22, till a few drops of water reach the receiver (C) of ammonia. The gas dissolves so rapidly in the water that a partial vacuum is formed, and the outside atmospheric pressure acting through A B produces the "ammonia fountain." The water turns blue as it enters the receiver.

Ammonia is a colorless gas, with *pungent* odor. It is much *lighter* than air. It is **very soluble** in water, 700 gals. dissolving in a single gallon of water at 15° (1000 vols. at 0°, see coal gas). It not only dissolves, but unites with water

Reaction:—

$H_3N + H_2O = H_4N\,HO$

forming ammonium hydrate ("ammonia water," hartshorn, etc.).

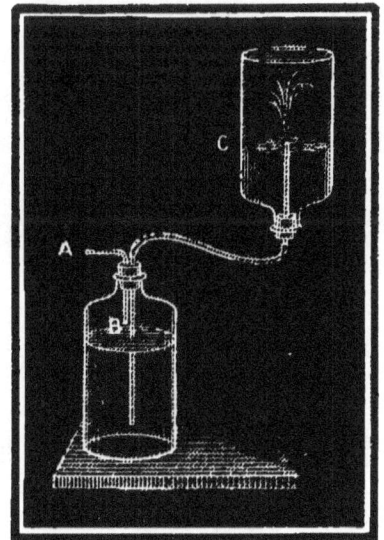

Fig. 22.—Ammonia Fountain.

The ammonium grouping can be passed from compound to compound like an element, and hence is a compound radical. (See AMMONIUM.) In concentrated "ammonia water" there is probably a large excess of the gas dissolved (more than unites with the water). Ammonium hydrate (or ammonia in the presence of moisture) has a strong alkaline reaction. It has been called the "volatile alkali," because its effect upon vegetable colors is only temporary. Prove this by dipping red litmus paper into dilute ammonia water and noticing that the red color returns again after a few hours. When the color of cloth, stained by an acid, has been restored by "ammonia water," the ammonium salt should be thoroughly washed out with water, or the red spot returns. (See CHEMISTRY OF CLEANING.)

"**Evaporation cools.**" This means that when a substance evaporates it absorbs heat from what is near by. (See sulphur dioxide, APPENDIX.) Wet one hand and pass both hands rapidly through the air. The wet hand is sensibly colder from the evaporation of the water. Pour a little ether upon the thermometer bulb. The ether quickly evaporates and the mercury falls.

A pressure of about $4\frac{1}{2}$ atmospheres (at 0°) converts gaseous into liquid ammonia. The evaporation of liquid ammonia produces intense cold (—40°). Advantage is taken in the arts of this fact to produce ice artificially.

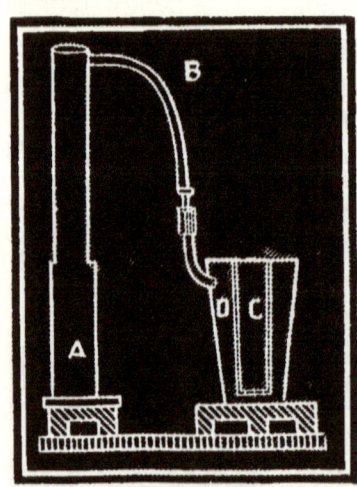
Fig. 23.—Ice Machine.

In a strong generator, A, is placed ice water saturated with ammonia gas (1,000 vols. in one). This is connected with an equally strong receiver D, by the tube B. Receiver D is placed in cold water. Heat is applied to A and the great pressure of escaping gas converts the gas into a liquid in D. Water is now placed in vessel C. Generator A is cooled and the liquid ammonia in D evaporates and is reabsorbed by water in A. The evaporation produces sufficient cold (takes away or absorbs sufficient heat) *to freeze water in* C. Other substances than ammonia may be used for this purpose, all, however, involving the principle of evaporation.

Nitrogen and hydrogen do not unite directly to form ammonia, but when decomposition is taking place in organic substances, and these two elements are leaving their old compounds, they unite. Elements just leaving their old compounds are said to be in the **nascent** state, and they have a much greater tendency to form new compounds.

CHAPTER XXI.

CARBON.

Carbon is a very abundant element. It forms a large proportion of vegetable and animal tissues, and is a prominent constituent of limestone, marble, etc. (**carbonates**). We know it in three allotropic states:—

1. **Diamond.**
2. **Graphite** (plumbago, black lead).
3. **Amorphous Carbon** (uncrystallized).

Graphite, mixed with a little Sb and S, is used to make common "lead pencils." Mixed with clay, it makes crucibles, the most *refractory* (difficult to melt, or of ores, difficult to reduce) known.

Amorphous Carbon (more or less impure) includes charcoal, mineral coal (the remains of vegetation of the carboniferous age), coke, peat, animal charcoal (bone black), soot, lamp-black, and gas-carbon.

NOTE.—For fuller description of the above and of all such substances briefly mentioned in this primary work, see the dictionary and cyclopædia. Every High School should have an unabridged dictionary and a cyclopædia *placed where scholars can readily refer to them.*

Carbon for a long time resists decay. Fence posts are charred to preserve them. Neither acids (except nitric) nor alkalies affect it.

Fig. 24.—Mercuric Tub.

EXP. 47.—Collect in test-tube over mercury (or by displacement of air) H_3N. Introduce into the gas a piece of fresh burned, dry charcoal, mounted on wire attached to perforated cork, and quickly dip the mouth of test-tube beneath mercury. The Hg rises in test-tube, because C absorbs the H_3N in its pores.

NOTE.—Chisel out of hard wood a trough 5 inches long, 1 inch wide, and 1 inch deep. Nail a lead post to one or both ends to support small test-tube. This makes a very good mercuric pneumatic tub, but the mercury must not come in contact with the lead. To avoid this the supports may be made of wood. Use narrow test-tubes and keep them from the side of the tub, else the air creeps in.

Carbon absorbs many times its bulk of gases, condensing them in its pores. Fresh burned charcoal is a good "**disinfectant**" for foul gases. They are destroyed within its pores by the absorbed O; *i. e.*, by oxidation (so that C is not a disinfectant in a strict *chemical* sense, but its action is mechanical). O is the real disinfectant.

EXP. 48.—Finely pulverize charcoal by rubbing two sticks together, or, if animal charcoal is used, by grinding in mortar, and place upon filter. Slowly moisten with distilled water. Let diluted ink (or indigo solution, vinegar, etc.) fall drop by drop upon the charcoal from an ordinary paper filter above it. The filtrate from charcoal is colorless.

Charcoal is a good **decolorizing agent.** Animal charcoal is largely used in sugar refineries to remove soluble impurities and color.

EXP. 49.—Heat upon platinum foil a piece of sugar (or other organic matter, as tartaric acid, flesh or vegetable). It chars (turns black, as the more volatile constituents are driven off, leaving the carbon free).

Charring is a good test for carbon (or for organic matter)

EXP. 50.—Upon charcoal put a little litharge (Pb O). Heat in the blow-pipe flame. The O is taken by the C leaving the Pb *free* (uncombined).

$$2\,Pb\,O + C = \underset{\text{metallic lead}}{Pb_2} + CO_2$$

Carbon is a good **deoxidizing** or **reducing agent.** Heated with the oxides of most metals it deoxidizes them, and is thus of special use in reducing ores that are oxides (or carbonates, since great heat breaks up the carbonate grouping, setting CO_2 free, and leaving an oxide behind).

EXP. 51.—Upon pieces of marble ($CaCO_3$) in a flask, pour dilute (20 per cent.) H Cl. Collect gas by displacement of air.

Reaction (class 4): $\underset{\text{carbonate}}{Ca\,CO_3} + \underset{\text{acid}}{2\,H\,Cl} = \underset{\text{salt}}{Ca\,Cl_2} + \underset{\text{water}}{H_2O} + \underset{\text{carbonic oxide}}{CO_2}$

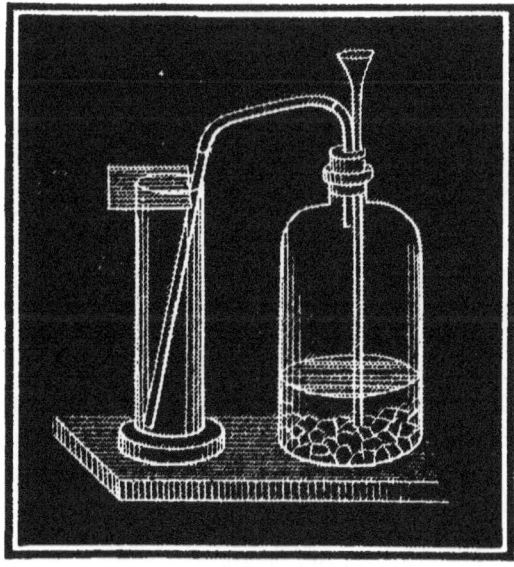

Fig. 25.

Carbon dioxide (carbonic oxide, carbonic anhydride, old name **carbonic acid**) is a colorless gas, with slightly acid taste. It is much **heavier** than the air (sp. gr. 1.5, with H as standard 22) in which it exists free, forming about $\frac{4}{10000}$ by volume.

Exp. 52.—Into a jar of CO_2 introduce a lighted taper. It is extinguished.

Exp. 53.—Arrange short lighted candles along an inclined (not too steep, else draft is produced) trough (piece of gutter). Pour a large receiver of CO_2 into the top of the trough. The candles go out in order as CO_2 reaches them.

Exp. 54.—Put a mouse into a receiver of CO_2. The animal dies.

Carbon dioxide does not support combustion and is **not inflammable.** Though not poisonous in a strict sense of the word, yet animals die from suffocation in air containing about five per cent. of the gas. It hinders the elimination of the same gas, CO_2 from the lungs (but see CO_2 in APPENDIX).

Exp. 55.—Burn Mg ribbon in a jar of CO_2. Black particles of carbon appear mixed with the white oxide.

$$CO_2 + Mg_2 = 2\underset{\text{white}}{MgO} + \underset{\text{black}}{C}$$

Dissolve oxide in dilute HNO_3 and C is made more distinct. CO_2 supports the combustion of magnesium, but by a supporter of combustion in general we mean a substance that supports the combustion of hydrocarbons.

Exp. 56.—Repeat Exp. 33.

Lime-water is the test for CO_2. No other gas will (1) extinguish flame and (2) render lime-water milky.

Exp. 57.—Hold the breath a short time and then expel the air into a receiver. Test. It extinguishes the flame of taper and turns lime-water, shaken up in the receiver, milky.

CARBON. 67

Animals exhale CO_2 from the lungs as a waste product. They use up O from the air and replace it by CO_2.

Fig. 26.

EXP. 58.—Place a small branch having numerous and fresh leaves in a tall receiver (prepared as in Fig. 26) of spring or brook water (*i. e.*, water that has been sufficiently exposed to carry much air dissolved) and place apparatus a few hours in direct sunshine. O is evolved and, together with a little N and traces of CO_2 driven off by the sun's heat (of course a little O is also driven off by sun's heat), collects in top of receiver. Test by very slender and glowing taper. The gas is found to be principally oxygen.

Plants in sunshine exhale through their leaves O (except certain low orders), using up CO_2 of the air and building the C into their tissues. The leaves of plants are often compared to the lungs of animals, except we must remember that the process is reverse. They receive the air through little stomata (mouths) on the under side (principally). But in some important respects the leaves correspond to the digestive organs of animals (including glands preparing chyle for the general circulation, viz., "mesenteric glands" and the liver). The plant gets vastly more food (by weight) from the air than from the richest soil. The smaller portion which it gets from the soil is, however, an *essential* portion, and it will not flourish in poor soil.

Plants purify the air for animals, and animals by a reverse process supply from their own waste the needed elements of plant food. Carbon dioxide is also formed in large quantities by the decay of organic matter. The proportion, however, of CO_2 in the air remains practically the same from year to year.

CO_2 tends to collect in old wells and in unventilated portions of mines. It is called by miners **choke-damp**. Wherever a light is extinguished by CO_2, it is unsafe to go.

EXP. 59.—Place a short lighted candle on a rubber cork and introduce it into the bottom of a vertical glass tube, which the cork fits. The candle goes out. In the tube suspend a smaller tube and introduce the lighted candle as before. It burns steadily. The heated air (and CO_2) rises in the small tube (upward draft) and the fresh air containing O falls between it and the larger tube.

Two openings, at least, are necessary for proper ventilation. In mines where it is possible, two shafts, one at each end, with a fire at the base of either, answers the purpose. Very complex arrangements, however, have to be made in many cases to force air into the various parts of large mines. Plenty of fresh air is the only preventive to keep fire-damp (marsh gas CH_4) and CO_2 from accumulating in dangerous quantities.

EXP. 60.—Hold the breath a short time and then expel it into a jar and close by rubber cork. Set aside in a warm place for a day or two and then open. A very offensive, putrescent odor greets the sweetest-breathed experimenter. (CO_2 has no odor.) [This experiment may, perhaps, best be performed at home.]

Churches, school-rooms, bedrooms, etc., should be very thoroughly ventilated, not so much to free them from the injurious CO_2 as to remove the **poisonous "animal vapor"** (moisture in suspension) thrown off from the lungs. This "vapor" holds all manner of organic impurities in solution.

EXP. 61.—Fill a narrow, deep test-tube with CO_2. Close with the thumb and open under cold water (but previously boiled), pressing the mouth a few inches below the surface. Close the test-tube, remove and shake. Part of the CO_2 dissolves. Open under water and repeat shaking. In this way the test-tube of CO_2 may be dissolved in a test-tube of water.

Water at 15° dissolves one vol. of CO_2, but if the gas is under pressure, it dissolves much more (by weight).

CARBON. 69

"**Soda Water**" is nothing but a solution of CO_2 under pressure in water. It probably receives its inappropriate name because of its effervescence when relieved of pressure (like sodium carbonate, "soda," when mixed with an acid).

CO_2 has been condensed to a liquid, and by rapid evaporation of a part, the rest is solidified (frozen), forming a snow-white solid. This solid is so cold that when touched it produces the same effect as red-hot iron (see similar condensation of SO_2, APPENDIX).

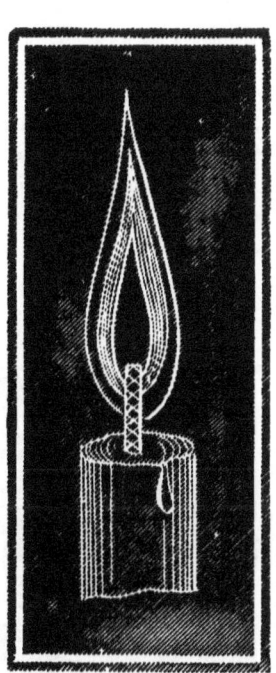

Fig. 27.

As we have seen, CO_2 and H_2O are the two great products of ordinary combustion. The chemistry of a burning candle is in a general sense very simple. The wick is first raised to the igniting point, the heat melts the tallow (composed chiefly of H and C combined), and the liquid is then drawn up by capillary attraction into the wick. Here the great heat changes the liquid tallow into the gaseous state (with decomposition into various hydrocarbons). *Flame is burning gas.* The flame is hollow, as no O can penetrate to its center, and the hollow is filled with the unburnt gases. (These may be drawn away by a fine glass tube and burned at its end, if the candle is a large one.) In floating outward, the C from the decomposed hydrocarbons becomes white hot and gives out light, but soon meets the O of the air and becomes CO_2 at the instant it ceases to give light. Outside is a faintly blue cone, cup-shaped at the bottom and composed of burning H (and CO). If a cold piece of glass or porcelain is introduced into the flame, the C is lowered below the igniting point and is deposited as smut. The H_2O (steam) is condensed and deposited also. We notice this condensed steam upon the cold chimney when the lamp is first lighted, but it evaporates as the chimney becomes hot.

Illuminating gas is made from bituminous coal by heating in retorts and collecting volatile hydrocarbons in a holder. It contains various gases, H, C O, C H_4 (**marsh gas,** "fire damp" of miners), C_2H_4 (**olefiant gas,** ethylene), C_6H_6 (vapor of benzol), etc., and (before purification) others that must be removed, as H_3N, C O_2, H_2S (and other sulphur compounds), besides vapor of "tar." Tar is a very complex substance, from which the aniline dyes, carbolic acid, etc., are obtained. H_3N may be removed by passing through water (or H Cl, old method), C O_2 by passing through "pans" of lime (Ca O), and the sulphur compounds by passing over ferric hydrate. The last reaction may be represented thus:—

$$Fe_2\ 6\ H\ O\ +\ H_2S\ =\ 2\ Fe\ 2\ H\ O\ +\ 2\ H_2O\ +\ S$$
ferric hydrate   hydrogen sulphide   ferrous hydrate   water   free sulphur

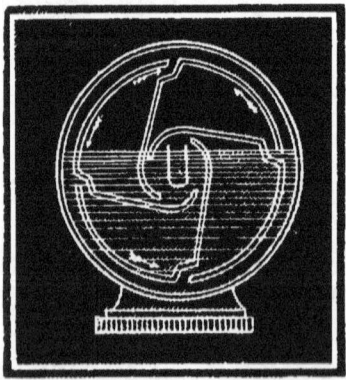

Fig. 23.—Section of Gas Meter.
The three arrows represent the rotation of the chambers; the solitary arrow the escape of the gas from chamber. Gas enters through the U-shaped center.

On exposure to the air, ferrous hydrate becomes ferric hydrate, and the material may be repeatedly used till the free sulphur forms from 40 to 50 per cent. The tar vapor condenses and runs into the "tar well." The refuse (coke) is left behind in the retorts.

The purified gas is measured by the meter and passes into the holder, from which it is distributed to consumers. Illuminating gas is also made from crude petroleum, more complex machinery being used.

Bunsen's Burner is represented in Fig. 21 and is used when *heat,* not light, is wanted. The gas is mixed with the air, drawn in through openings at the side. The flame is condensed, is much hotter, and does not smut cold glass.

CARBON. 71

EXP. 62.—Heat in extreme tip of blowpipe flame the end of a clean copper wire. It turns black, i. e., is oxidized, forming Cu O. Heat in the midst of flame nearer the blowpipe. The Cu O is reduced (deoxidized) and the bright metallic copper appears.

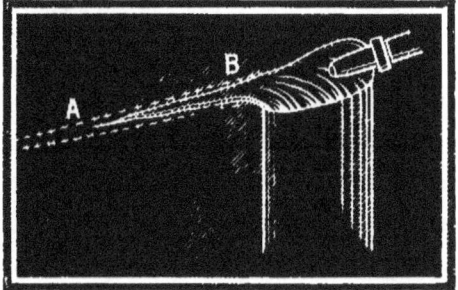
Fig. 29.

By means of the **blowpipe** we may do *two* things **oxidize** most metals (a very small portion is sufficient for tests) and **reduce** their oxides.

At A (Fig. 29) a substance may be oxidized, because here we have an excess of O thrown forward from the blowpipe and highly heated. The flame in the center at B is reducing, for here there is an excess of highly heated carbon. The reducing flame is best produced by holding the nozzle of blowpipe a very short distance from the flame instead of in it. The **blowpipe** is a very valuable instrument in the **analysis of ores.**

EXP. 63.—Two inches above a gas burner hold a fine wire gauze and ignite jet of gas above the gauze. It burns above, but not below. The wire being a good conductor of heat reduces the gas below the igniting point, and the flame cannot pass through the gauze.

Davy's Safety Lamp used by miners is essentially a lamp surrounded by a wire gauze. The flame cannot pass through this to ignite the "fire-damp" (CH_4 marsh gas). This dangerous gas explodes violently when mixed with air and ignited.

EXP. 64.—Into a flask put a small quantity of oxalic acid crystals and cover with strong sulphuric acid. Heat gently and pass gases through wash bottle containing strong solution of K H O. Collect over water.

$$H_2C_2O_4 = H_2O + C\overset{\nearrow}{O_2} + C\overset{\nearrow}{O}$$

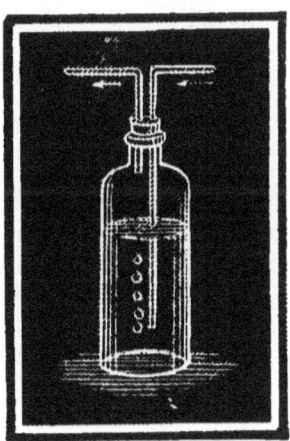
Fig. 30.—Wash Bottle.

The sulphuric acid absorbs H_2O from the oxalic acid, breaking up the molecule. The K H O solution absorbs the CO_2, becoming K_2CO_3 (and H_2O), and the C O is collected in receiver. Test by lighted taper. It burns with bluish flame.

Carbon monoxide C O (carb*o*n*ous* oxide, old name carbonic oxide) is a colorless **poisonous** gas formed by burning C in a close atmosphere. Escaping from hot stoves through the pores of the iron into ill-ventilated rooms, it causes headache. In large quantities it speedily produces coma and death. Its pale, lambent flame is frequently seen when fresh hard coal is placed upon the grate.

NOTE.—**Organic chemistry** may be considered as *carbon continued* The previous rules for writing formulas and names, which hold so generally in inorganic chemistry, fail in numberless instances to meet the requirements of organic chemistry, as we shall see. Notice that the order of C H and O is usually used in organic chemistry instead of H C and O. (See marsh gas, vapor of benzol, etc., above, and also ORGANIC CHEMISTRY.)

CHAPTER XXII.

BINARY ACID- AND SALT-FORMERS

FLUORINE, CHLORINE, BROMINE, IODINE, AND CYANOGEN.

EXP. 65.—Into a small flask on a sand-bath, put equal weights of common salt and manganese dioxide, well mixed. Add sufficient water to make thin paste. Pour in through funnel a small quantity of sulphuric acid (commercial) and collect gas in large test-tube over hot water, or by displacement of air in *deep* receivers. Heat should be applied to flask to drive off the last (and greater portion) of the gas. A double reaction takes place:—

(1)—$H_2SO_4 + 2NaCl = Na_2SO_4 + 2HCl$

(2)—$MnO_2 + 4HCl = MnCl_2 + 2H_2O + Cl_2$

BINARY ACID- AND SALT-FORMERS. 73

The gas may be freed from H Cl by passing through wash bottle (see Fig. 30) of cold water. It may be dried, if desired, by passing through strong $H_2S O_4$ in the same manner, and then collected by displacement of air.

Caution.—Care should be taken not to breathe (except in minute quantities) chlorine, cyanogen, or, in short, any gases or products that are poisonous. Small quantities of such gases should be used in experiments. If larger quantities are desired, they should be made under a "gas chimney," or near a window with outward draft.

Chlorine is a *greenish-yellow, poisonous gas* of a suffocating odor. When very dilute it produces coughing (relieved by inhaling dilute ammonia), and breathed in larger quantities, inflammation of the trachea and bronchial tubes. It is **2.5** times heavier than air. It is an abundant element, but is not found free in nature.

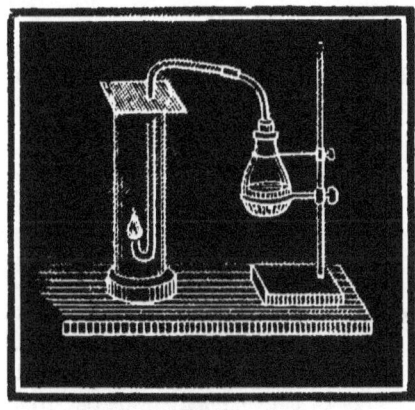

Fig. 31.

EXP. 66.—Burn a jet of H in Cl and test product by blue litmus. (Fig. 31.)

$$H + Cl = HCl$$

EXP. 67.—Into a jar of Cl plunge a small lighted *pitch-wood* taper. It burns awhile with red, smoky flame, but soon goes out. The Cl unites with H of the taper, setting the C free as smoke. Test by blue litmus.

Cl has a great affinity for H. Upon this affinity depends its value as a **disinfectant.** H is an essential constituent of many foul gases. Cl destroys them as it destroys coloring matters. (See EXP. 72.)

EXP. 68.—Upon paper containing printer's ink write with common ink (iron tannate Fe_3 2 $C_{27}H_{19}O_{17}$) and lower into a jar of Cl. The common ink is bleached, but the printer's ink (linseed oil and lamp-black, C) is unaffected.

Exp. 69.—Into a black bottle containing cold water pass Cl gas (purified of H Cl). The Cl dissolves (3 vols.) and forms "chlorine water." Set aside as a reagent.

Exp. 70.—Expose a little chlorine water in a beaker to the sunlight for a few hours. Place it beside a beaker of fresh chlorine water from dark bottle, and to each add a piece of blue litmus paper. The fresh chlorine water bleaches, the other turns the litmus red. The light enabled the Cl to decompose the water thus:—

$$Cl_2 + H_2O = 2\,H\,Cl + O$$

("Light favors chemical change.")

Exp. 71.—Into a beaker containing Cl water let fall a few drops of red ink (cochineal), or indigo solution, aniline purple, etc. The color is discharged.

Exp. 72.—Into a beaker of chlorine water introduce a piece of calico. The color is discharged, except from those portions colored by mineral substances.

Chlorine is a powerful **bleaching agent,** and for this purpose is largely used in the arts. It bleaches (and disinfects) in two ways:—

1. By removing H from the substance.
2. By removing H from water, setting free "nascent" O, which bleaches. (Thus Cl bleaches *by proxy.*) Dry Cl does not bleach.

Bleaching powder, "chloride of lime," is mixture of calcium hypochlorite (Ca 2 Cl O) and calcium chloride (Ca Cl_2). A dilute acid sets chlorine free with promptness. Moisture and exposure sets chlorine free slowly, therefore bleaching powder is used as a disinfectant. Acids set the chlorine free rapidly. Cl may be conveniently prepared from bleaching powder.

Exp. 73.—Into a jar of Cl sprinkle antimony (powdered with a file). It takes fire and fills the jar with white fumes. (Sb Cl_5, poisonous.)

Exp. 74.—Burn Mg ribbon in jar of Cl, igniting it first in alcohol or Bunsen's flame.

Cl has a great affinity for the metals. (Sb is semi-metal.) Most of them burn in chlorine, forming chlorides. Chlorine, as we have seen, does not unite with carbon and

BINARY ACID- AND SALT-FORMERS. 75

therefore does not support the combustion of hydrocarbons.

EXP. 75.—Into a test-tube containing a little common salt, pour strong sulphuric acid, and gently heat. Collect gas in narrow, deep test-tube by displacement of air (holding mouth upward).

$$2\,NaCl + H_2SO_4 = Na_2SO_4 + 2\,HCl$$

Cover test-tube with thumb and open under water; the water rushes in violently and fills the tube.

Hydrochloric acid (hydrogen chloride, chlorohydric acid, muriatic acid) is a colorless, irrespirable, acid **gas, very soluble in water** (450 vols. in one at 15°). The liquid called hydrochloric acid is really a solution of the gas in water (a mere solution).

EXP. 76.—Dip a glass rod into strong ammonia water, and another into strong H Cl and bring the rods together. Dense white fumes of ammonium chloride appear. The reaction is:—

$$H_4N\,HO + HCl = H_4NCl + H_2O$$

or omitting the water

$$H_3N + HCl = H_4NCl$$

This is a rough *test* for H Cl or for *free* ammonia.

EXP. 77.—Boil in H Cl a small piece of gold-leaf. It does not dissolve. Add a drop of H N O₃, a yellow solution of gold chloride (AuCl₃) appears.

Hydrochloric acid and nitric acid form **aqua regia,** the solvent of gold.

EXP. 78.—Repeat EXP. 6 and 7, and also use other soluble chlorides. Soluble chlorides precipitate silver as silver chloride.

EXP. 79.—Heat a little pulverized K Cl O₃ upon charcoal in the blowpipe flame. The coal burns explosively.

$$2\,KClO_3 + C_3 = 2\,KCl + 3\,CO_2$$

The **chlorates,** as well as the **nitrates,** are good **oxidizing agents.** Potassium chlorate is one of the most important of the chlorates.

Exp. 80.—In a test-tube thoroughly mix a little pulverized K Br and Mn O_2, moisten with water, add strong H_2SO_4, quickly close by perforated rubber cork and collect liquid in deep test-tube cooled in water. (Exp. 39.) Heat to drive off the larger portion of the bromine. Pour into glass-stoppered bottle and preserve.

(1)—H_2SO_4 + 2 K Br = K_2SO_4 + 2 H Br

(2)—Mn O_2 + 4 H Br = Mn Br_2 + 2 H_2O + Br_2

Bromine is a *volatile, poisonous*, dark red **liquid**, very similar in its properties to chlorine, but less active.

Many experiments analogous to those under Cl may be performed with bromine vapor. Thus, Br **bleaches** and unites with H to form hydrobromic acid. H Br and other soluble bromides precipitate silver as *yellow* silver bromide, which blackens in sunlight like silver chloride. (Perform experiments and write reactions.) Br is not a very abundant element. Potassium bromide is used in medicine to repress excessive reflex action (nervousness, hysterics, etc.).

Exp. 81.—Into a test-tube put solution of K Br and add a drop or two of chlorine water.

Reaction: K Br + Cl = K Cl + Br (free)

The solution becomes yellow. Bromine water is yellow.

This experiment shows the superior **chemism (chemical affinity)** or activity of chlorine and a method of testing for bromides.

Exp. 82.—In a deep test-tube place pulverized K I and Mn O_2 well mixed. Moisten, and adding strong H_2SO_4, gently heat. *Violet colored* vapor of iodine appears. Set aside for a few moments. Iodine condenses on the sides of the test-tube.

Iodine is a grayish-black *solid* with metallic luster. It is a comparatively rare element.

Exp. 83.—To tincture (*solution in alcohol*) of iodine *very dilute* (with water), add *dilute* solution of starch paste. *Blue* iodide of starch appears. [That the compound is not a very stable one may be shown by gently heating. The blue color disappears, but reappears as the solution cools.]

BINARY ACID- AND SALT-FORMERS. 77

Exp. 84.—Boil a small piece of potato in beaker of water. Filter, and, after filtrate is *cold*, add a few drops of very dilute iodine tincture. Blue iodide of starch appears.

Starch is a very delicate **test** for *free* iodine, and, *vice versa*, iodine for starch. (See Exp. 85.)

Soluble iodides precipitate silver as silver iodide, which blackens in sunlight. Iodine was formerly much used in medicine to "scatter" glandular swellings, etc. It is now less often used.

Exp. 85.—Into a test-tube put solution of K I. Add two or three drops of starch solution. No *blue* color appears, because the I is combined with K. Add a few drops of chlorine water. The *blue* color appears because the Cl unites with the K setting the I free.

$$K I + Cl = K Cl + I \text{ (free)}$$

The free I then unites with the starch, forming the *blue* color.

This experiment shows the superior **chemical affinity** of chlorine and a method of testing for iodides.

Fluorine is the only element which does not unite chemically with oxygen. It is supposed to be a colorless gas, but so great is its **chemical affinity** that it has not been satisfactorily isolated (set free).

Exp. 86.—In a platinum or lead crucible place two grams of pulverized Fluor Spar (Ca F_2) and cover with strong $H_2S O_4$. Coat a piece of glass at a gentle heat with paraffine (or wax) and having written a word upon the paraffine, gently heat crucible, and removing lamp, cover with glass. The word is etched upon the glass. (**Caution,** Exp. 65.)

$$(1)—Ca F_2 + H_2S O_4 = Ca S O_4 + 2 H F$$

$$(2)—4 H F + \underset{\substack{\text{of the} \\ \text{glass (which see)}}}{Si O_2} = 2 H_2O + Si F_4$$

Hydrofluoric acid (H F) is used for **etching** letters or designs upon glass. If the gas is used, the letters or designs are left rough· but if a solution of the gas in water (kept in *gutta percha bottles*) is used, the etched portion is smooth.

CHEMICAL PRIMER.

Exp. 87.—In a tube of hard glass place a small quantity of mercuric cyanide (Hg 2 C N). Heat carefully to dull redness and collect gas in test-tube over mercury. Test by lighted taper. The gas burns with beautiful reddish-purple flame. **(Caution,** Exp. 65.)

$$(1) - Hg\, 2\, C\, N = Hg + (C\, N)_2$$
$$(2) - C\, N + O_2 = C\, O_2 + N$$

Cyanogen (C N or Cy) is a colorless, pungent, inflammable gas with strong *peach-blossom* odor. As the molecule of hydrogen has been represented thus $\boxed{H\,H}$, so the molecule of free cyanogen may be represented thus $\boxed{C\,N\,C\,N}$ or C_2N_2.

It is interesting as being the first **"compound radical"** isolated. It forms binary salts, several of which are very important. The intensely poisonous "prussic" acid (hydro-cyanic acid, H C N) may be formed by the action of sulphuric acid on potassium cyanide. *(Do not perform the experiment.)*

$$2\,K\,C\,N + H_2S\,O_4 = K_2S\,O_4 + 2\,H\,C\,N$$

Prussic acid is used in medicine. Many patent medicines claiming to be preparations from cherry bark are essentially nothing but very dilute solutions of hydro-cyanic acid. Potassium cyanide is one of the most important of the cyanides. It is *very poisonous*.

MISCELLANEOUS QUESTIONS.

1. Reactions in making O?
2. How many litres of O can be made from 150 grams of K Cl O_3? [Note.—**A litre of H weighs .0896 grams** (at 0° and barometer 760 mm), and a litre of O weighs 16 times as much, a litre of N 14 times as much, etc., according to the *atomic weight of the gas*. To find the weight of compound gases, *multiply the weight of H by one-half the molecular weight of the gas*. Ex.—A litre of C O_2 weighs 22 times .0896 gms.]
3. Tell what you know about O (ten lines).
4. Give experiments proving the character (properties) of O.
5. Reaction in making H?
6. How many litres of H could be made by using 5 grams of Zn?
7. How many grams of Zn must be used to make 15 litres of H?

8. Give properties of H and prove by detailing experiments.
9. What is a deliquescent salt? An efflorescent salt?
10. How was N obtained?
11. Give the composition of air.
12. What was proved by the "ammonia fountain"?
13. What is "aqua regia"? and why so called?
14. What is meant by "nascent" hydrogen?
15. Give experiment proving that C is a good decolorizing agent.
16. Give experiment showing that *fresh burned* C is good "disinfectant"
17. How may CO_2 be made?
18. Fifty litres of CO_2 could be made by using what quantity (grams) of $Mg\,CO_3$?
19. Detail three experiments under carbonic oxide.
20. Animals and the higher orders of plants differ with respect to use of CO_2 and O. How?
21. Write 5 lines about chlorine, saying the most possible.
22. How is glass etched? Copper and iron?
23. What is cyanogen? Why is it treated in the chapter on chlorine, bromine, etc., rather than under nitrogen or carbon?

CHAPTER XXIII.

SULPHUR AND PHOSPHORUS.

Sulphur is found free (native) *in volcanic regions.* It is found combined in cinnabar (Hg S), iron pyrites (Fe S_2 iron disulphide), galena (Pb S), blende (Zn S), etc. It is contained in most animal tissues and especially in the perspiration and hair, also in many vegetables, especially in those that are strong-smelling.

EXP. 88.—Drop a well-cleaned silver coin upon yolk of egg and leave over night. It is blackened.

Eggs contain sulphur and so tarnish silver spoons, *black* silver sulphide (Ag_2S) being formed.

EXP. 89.—Into a strong solution of lead acetate introduce white horse-hairs, and heat to hasten reaction. They turn dark.

Many "hair dyes" contain salts of lead. The metal unites with S of the hair, forming *black* Pb S. Such hair dyes are highly injurious.

Sulphur exists in several allotropic *(physically different)* states, among which are (1) the crystallized, (2) the common uncrystallized ("amorphous"), and (3) the plastic (viscid, also uncrystallized).

EXP. 90.—Heat a small quantity of sulphur for about five minutes, or till the thin, light-colored melted mass, after becoming dark and thick, becomes thin again. Pour by thin stream into cold water. Plastic S results. This form is unstable and becomes brittle in a day or two, as may be proved by examining specimen the next morning.

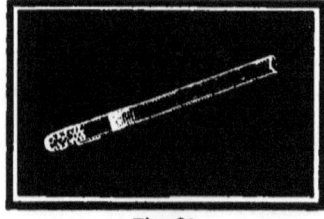

Fig. 32.

EXP. 91.—In a small glass tube closed at one end (by fusing tip in flame of Bunsen's burner) place small piece of iron pyrites (FeS_2) and heat *slowly* so as not to crack the fused end of tube. Part of the sulphur sublimes and condenses on cold part of the tube.

$$3 FeS_2 = Fe_3S_4 + S_2$$

NOTE.—A substance *sublimes* when, on applying heat, it rises as a vapor and condenses as a solid. A substance *distills* when it rises as a vapor and condenses as a liquid.

S may be obtained from iron pyrites by "roasting" the ore and condensing the S. The principal supply, however, comes from the volcanic regions of Italy. (See EXP. 93.)

EXP. 92.—Repeat EXP. 4, placing in the bottle a red rose. The rose is slowly bleached.

SULPHUR AND PHOSPHORUS. 81

Sulphur dioxide is used in **bleaching** *silk, straw*, and *woolen* goods, which would be injured (turned yellow) by chlorine. Colorless compounds are formed by the union of the SO_2 with the coloring matter, but the reaction is too complex to be written out.

SO_2 is also an **antiseptic.** S burned in a vessel prevents the fermentation of the liquid (as new cider) afterwards put in. Like all strong antiseptics it is poisonous.

EXP. 93.—Burn S in a large, clean flask and pass into it H_2S. (See EXP. 8.) Let stand a few hours—the bottom and sides of the flask are covered with a thin *white* coat of sulphur. [S looks white when in thin deposit.]

$$SO_2 + 2H_2S = S_3 + 2H_2O$$

This illustrates the formation of native sulphur *in volcanic regions*, as volcanic gases contain SO_2 and H_2S.

EXP. 94.—Burn S as in EXP. 4, and quickly stir with glass rod, upon the end of which is twine wet with strong HNO_3. (*Nitrates* are good *oxidizing agents*, we have learned.) The SO_2 takes O from the nitric acid, becoming SO_3 sulphuric oxide (anhydride). Shake up with water.

$$SO_3 + H_2O = H_2SO_4 \text{ (dilute)}$$

Test water with barium chloride, the test of sulphuric acid (and soluble sulphates).

$$H_2SO_4 + BaCl_2 = \underset{\text{white precipitate}}{BaSO_4} + 2HCl$$

Sulphuric acid ("oil of vitriol") is a colorless (if pure) *oily liquid* (sp. gr. 1.84). It is the *most important* of the acids, and is used in preparing numberless other substances, especially acids.

The experiment illustrates its preparation.

SO_2 from burning sulphur is carried into large leaden chambers, whose floors are covered with water. Into these air and nitric acid fumes are admitted. The N_2O_2 from the nitric acid acts as a carrier of O from the air to the SO_2. (See Exp. 38.)

$$2SO_2 + N_2O_4 = 2SO_3 + N_2O_2$$

$$N_2O_2 + \underset{\substack{\text{from} \\ \text{the air}}}{O_2} = N_2O_4$$

The dilute acid is evaporated in leaden pans, till it begins to attack the lead. (Commercial H_2SO_4 contains $PbSO_4$, which falls as white precipitate when the acid is diluted.) It is then removed and concentrated in glass or platinum stills.

Exp. 95.—Into a beaker containing water pour twice its volume of strong H_2SO_4. Great heat is developed.

Exp. 96.—Upon white sugar ($C_{12}H_{22}O_{11}$) (starch or wood $C_6H_{10}O_5$) pour strong sulphuric acid. It chars by removing the elements of water, leaving the black carbon free.—Evaporate dilute H_2SO_4 upon white paper. As the acid increases in strength, the paper chars.

Concentrated sulphuric acid has a *great affinity for water*. It is used for drying gases with which it does not react. Care must be taken in diluting the acid, to mix in a vessel that will stand the **heat.** (In diluting heavy liquids, pour the liquid into the water, not water into the liquid.) *"Fuming sulphuric acid"* is a solution of SO_3 in H_2SO_4.

Exp. 97.—Into a solution (slightly acidulated with HCl) of salts of lead, copper, bismuth, mercury (ic), arsenicum, antimony, and tin respectively in test-tubes, put solution of H_2S. Reaction by change of partners throws down sulphides. PbS black, CuS black, Bi_2S_3 black, HgS white, yellow, reddish-brown, and finally black, As_2S_3 lemon yellow, Sb_2S_3 orange, SnS brownish-black, SnS_2 yellow.

Hydrogen sulphide (H_2S "sulphuretted hydrogen") is much used in the **laboratory** to precipitate metals, as sulphides. (See Analytical Charts.) H_2S is readily inflammable, as may be shown by igniting in test-tube.

SULPHUR AND PHOSPHORUS. 83

NOTE.—Hydrogen sulphide has a slight acid reaction and was called by the old chemists *hydrosulphuric acid*. It unites with many of the bases to form sulphides, and these sulphides might be classed as binary salts. For reasons which need not be explained here, chemists do not now class sulphides in this way, but consider them as analogous to oxides.

Carbon disulphide ($C S_2$), a volatile, colorless, inflammable liquid, may be produced by passing sulphur over red-hot coals. It is an excellent **solvent,** dissolving readily S, P, I, and many organic substances. It **refracts light** powerfully, and hence is often used in filling prisms. The impure disulphide (its heavy vapor) is used to poison squirrels, insects, etc.

The rare element, selenium, in many respects resembles sulphur. We have the compounds H_2Se, $Se O_2$, $H_2Se O_4$, etc. (See SULPH- AND SELEN-SALTS.)

Phosphorus is a semi-transparent, nearly colorless, wax-like solid. It is kept under water in "sticks," as it slowly oxidizes in the air and takes fire at a very low temperature. It is highly poisonous. Its vapor breathed (in more than minute quantities) produces ulceration of the jaw, cured with difficulty. (See CAUTION, EXP. 24.)

Another variety, red or amorphous, is known. This differs widely from ordinary P. It does not emit the "jaw-poisoning fumes" and can be safely handled. P in this "allotropic" state may be prepared by heating ordinary phosphorus in a closed vessel. Part of the P used in making N (EXP. 35) is changed into the red variety.

Phosphorus, because of its low igniting point, is largely used in the manufacture of **matches.** The wood of the match is first dipped in melted sulphur, then into paste of P, potassium nitrate (or chlorate) for an oxidizing agent and glue (varnish). The P is kindling for the S, the S for the wood (hydrocarbon), while the nitrate furnishes the O for rapid combustion. The reactions in burning a match are:—

$$P_2 + O_5 = P_2O_5; \quad S + O_2 = SO_2;$$
$$H_2 + O = H_2O; \quad C + O_2 = CO_2.$$

"**Safety Matches**" contain no P, and ignite readily only when the chemicals of the match are rubbed on a surface of red phosphorus (and powdered glass to increase friction).

Phosphorus glows in the dark (its best test). (See APPENDIX.) Such glowing without heat is called **phosphorescence,** but not by any means is all so-called "phosphorescence" produced by phosphorus.

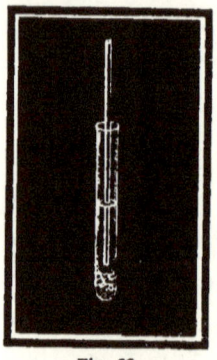

Fig. 33.

EXP. 98.—Into a test-tube half full of water drop several very small pieces of P. Cover P with fine crystals of $KClO_3$ (oxidizing agent). By means of a pipette (glass tube) take up a little strong H_2SO_4, and, introducing the tube into the water as deep as the $KClO_3$ (Fig. 33), open, letting the strong acid upon the chlorate. The P burns beneath the water.

A combustible element burns if raised to the igniting point in presence of free oxygen, or of an oxidizing agent. (In this case Cl_2O_4 from the reaction.)

Calcium phosphate ($Ca_3 2 PO_4$) forms fully one-half by weight of bones, and is the source of P. "Superphosphate of lime" is a peculiar acid phosphate of calcium ($CaH_4 2 PO_4$).

CHAPTER XXIV.

BORON AND SILICON.

Boron may be obtained from boron oxide B_2O_3 as a *brown powder*, and also in yellowish-brown crystals. **Boracic acid,** or boric acid (H_3BO_3), is found in the lagoons of the volcanic regions of Tuscany. Jets of steam containing the acid issue from the earth and are absorbed by the water. This is afterward evaporated by heat from the jets, leaving the crystallized acid. Boracic acid is also made from borax.

Exp. 99.—Upon copper (or iron) wire covered with a coating of the black oxide, melt a borax bead. The melted borax *dissolves* the oxide, leaving the bright "metallic" copper (or iron).

Borax (sodium tetraborate, $Na_2 B_4O_7, 10H_2 O$) is used in welding and soldering, because when melted it dissolves the oxide of the metal, leaving the surfaces bright. (See HARD WATER.)

Exp. 100.—Dissolve boracic acid (or borax previously moistened by drop of dilute sulphuric acid, to liberate *boracic acid*) in a little alcohol ($C_2H_5 H O$) and ignite. The flame has a peculiar *green* tint. This is a good test for the presence of a borate.

Exp. 101.—Dissolve copper oxide in borax bead in oxidizing flame of the blowpipe. Color *green* when hot, *blue* when cold. Change to reducing flame, color, reddish-yellow. Dissolve $Mn O_2$, intense reddish-violet in oxidizing flame, in reducing flame almost colorless. (See BLOWPIPE, APPENDIX.)

Borax is largely used in **blowpipe analysis** as a "flux."

Silicon is, next to O, the most abundant element, though, unlike O, it is always found combined (not free or native). The larger part of the earth's crust is silicon

Fig. 31.—Quartz Crystal.

oxide (Si O_2 **silica,** white sand, **quartz**), or silicates. Many precious stones (amethyst, agate, etc.) are quartz colored with some metallic oxide. Silicates of K and Na, absorbed by roots, give by deposit of silica the stiffness and shining surface to corn-stocks and the edge of "sword grass." Quartz veins often "carry" more or less free gold, and silver.

Petrifaction is the *replacement* of wood by stone (silica). Silica and certain silicates are *soluble* in water containing alkaline (K, Na, H_4N) carbonates. As fast as the wood placed in the water decays, the silica is deposited, and copies very precisely the lines of the wood (knots, grain, etc.).

Glass is a mixture of several silicates (as is also porcelain). **Crown** or **plate glass** (common window glass) is chiefly calcium and sodium silicates. Ca hardens and gives luster. Na makes fusible, but gives greenish tint.

Bohemian glass is chiefly calcium and potassium silicates. Potassium gives no color.

Flint glass is chiefly K and Pb silicates. This can be ground into imitation gems, prisms, etc. When very rich in lead it is known as *"paste."*

EXP. 102.—Into a piece of soft glass fuse cobalt oxide (CoO), the piece is colored a deep blue.

Glass is **colored** any desired tint by fusing with a small quantity of some metallic oxide. "Purple of Cassius" (which see) is used for the finer *ruby red;* cuprous oxide also colors *red;* cupric, chromium, and ferrous oxides give *green;* cobalt oxide gives *blue.* arsenous oxide the white, soft enamel of lamp shades; manganese oxide *violet,* etc.

Glass is **annealed** by being cooled very gradually for days. When cooled quickly, it is very brittle. Lamp chimneys break from sudden change of temperature, because not properly annealed.

Glass is **etched** by hydrofluoric acid as we have seen in EXP. 86.

Pure clay (kaolin, china clay, $H_2 Al_2 Si_2 O_8 + H_2 O$) under the influence of heat forms a hard, porous solid. Pure feldspar ($K_2 Na_2 Al_2 Si_6 O_{16}$) when heated fuses to a colorless glass. If china clay and ground feldspar are heated together, the fused feldspar penetrates the porous, infusible clay, producing a hard, translucent, lustrous mass—**porcelain.** Besides the many well-known uses of porcelain, it is employed in the laboratory, as it resists the action of acids and is quite refractory.

Stoneware differs from porcelain in opacity, due to the fact that the fused, feldspathic glass does not penetrate the entire porous mass of clay.

In common earthenware a poorer clay is used. The glazing is done by throwing common salt (Na Cl) into the kiln when the burning is nearly complete. The salt volatilizes and chemical reactions produce sodium aluminum silicate, giving a glassy surface.

Common pottery ware ("brown earthen") is made of the most impure forms of clay, usually colored reddish-brown with ferric and other oxides. It is often glazed with "lead" by mixing lead oxide or galena (Pb S) with the clay.

Silicates (or silica) are most excellent substances to "make hills of," because of their insolubility and hardness. Evidently the earth's crust could not be made of soluble matter, nor could there be firm continents if the crust were made of soft material.

CHAPTER XXV.

ARSENICUM, ANTIMONY, AND CHROMIUM.

Arsenicum (sp. gr. 5.7) is a brittle, steel-gray solid (semi-metal), generally found in combination. Two sulphides, yellow, As_2S_3 (arsenous sulphide, orpiment) and red As_2S_2 (realgar), occur native.

Caution.—Care must be taken in experimenting with arsenicum, as itself and its compounds are violently poisonous. Use very small quantities in all experiments; especially avoid breathing H_3As. (See ANTIDOTES.)

EXP. 103.—Place in a small glass tube, closed at one end "white arsenic" (As_2O_3 arsenous oxide "**ratsbane**") of the bulk of a pin's head. Hold inclined and heat *very gradually* (more perfect crystals are formed than by rapid heating). The "arsenic" sublimes and condenses in minute, octahedral crystals in the upper and colder part of the tube. (Examine crystals with a lens.)

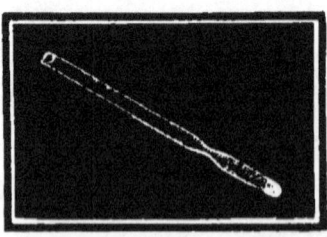

Fig. 35.

EXP. 104.—Perform EXP. 103 in a closed, drawn-out tube (Fig. 35), placing above the arsenous oxide (anhydride) powdered charcoal, and first raising the charcoal to low red heat. A dark mirror-like ring of arsenicum condenses upon the tube above, and a **garlic odor** is distinctly perceived. [If heating is too rapid the carbon is thrown up by draft. Though not so sharply defined, the arsenicum mirror, in case of this accident, is readily distinguished from the charcoal.]

$$2 As_2O_3 + C_3 = 3 CO_2 + As_4$$

Exp. 105.—Boil a few decigrams of "white arsenic" in water.

$$\underset{\substack{\text{acid-forming} \\ \text{oxide or} \\ \text{anhydride}}}{As_2O_3} + \underset{\text{water}}{3 H_2O} = \underset{\substack{\text{hydrogen} \\ \text{arsenite} \\ \text{(acid)}}}{2 H_3As O_3}$$

Filter and preserve filtrate as a sample of an arsen**ite**. (Of course this may be considered a solution of arsenous oxide in water. (See Exp. 11.)

Exp. 106.—Place a little of As_2O_3 of the bulk of a pin's head in ten drops of strong $H N O_3$, and, having raised to the boiling point, evaporate over water-bath nearly to dryness. Dilute with water, filter and preserve as an example of an arsen**ate**.

1. $\underset{\substack{\text{arsenous} \\ \text{oxide}}}{As_2O_3} + \underset{\substack{\text{from nitric} \\ \text{acid, an} \\ \text{oxidizing} \\ \text{agent}}}{O_2} = \underset{\substack{\text{arsenic} \\ \text{oxide}}}{As_2O_5}$

2. $\underset{\substack{\text{acid-forming} \\ \text{oxide}}}{As_2O_5} + \underset{\text{water}}{3 H_2O} = \underset{\text{acid}}{2 H_3As O_4}$

Exp. 107.—To copper sulphate solution (5 per cent.) add $H_4N H O$ till the precipitate formed is partially but not wholly dissolved. Filter, divide filtrate into two portions. To the first add drop by drop an arseni*te*, a *green* precipitate of acid copper arsenite ($H Cu As O_3$, "Scheele's Green," Paris green, etc., used as a pigment) falls. To the second portion add a few drops of an arsen*ate*, an acid copper arsenate ($H Cu As O_4$) bluish-*green*, falls. (See Acid-Salts.)

Exp. 108.— To silver nitrate solution ($2\frac{1}{2}$ per cent.) add $H_4N H O$ till precipitate is partially but not wholly dissolved. Filter, divide filtrate into two portions and proceed as in Exp. 107; from first portion *yellow* silver arsenite ($Ag_3 As O_3$) falls; from the second portion a beautiful *chocolate* silver arsenate ($Ag_3 As O_4$) falls. Add ammonium hydrate (or other moderately strong alkaline solution), each of the precipitates dissolve.

By the last experiment an arsenite may be readily distinguished from an arsenate. The pupil may learn here that the chemist in analysis depends largely upon the **color of precipitates** and **solubility** (or insolubility) in various reagents. (See Exps. 109 and 111.)

Arsenic acid is used in preparing aniline red (for dyeing), and other arsenates (especially $Na_3 As O_4$) are used in calico printing.

Fig. 36.

EXP. 109.—Into a small flask prepared with safety-funnel as in Fig. 36, and containing Zn, pour dilute H_2SO_4 and *after air is expelled* ignite as with philosopher's lamp. P ur through the funnel a few drops of arsenical solution (*ate* or *ite*). The color of the flame changes and the cold dish is smutted with arsenicum. (Just as a candle-flame smuts a cold dish with C. The arsenicum of the H_3As is lowered below the igniting point, while the hydrogen is not.) Upon the mirror-like spot place a drop of ~~calcium chloride~~ solution (or of hot strong nitric acid), it dissolves, unlike the antimonial spot. (See EXP. 111.)

(1)—$Zn + H_2SO_4 = ZnSO_4 + H_2$

(2)—H_3 + As = H_3As
"nascent" hydrogen   inflammable gas

(3)—$2 H_3As + O_6 = 3 H_2O + As_2O_3$
           from air

If a cold test-tube be placed over without touching the arsenical flame, octahedral and characteristic crystals of As_2O_3 and moisture condense upon its sides.

NOTE.—Don't breathe the gas H_3As. The experiment should be performed under a gas chimney or near a window with *outward* draft. If a small test-tube (without safety-funnel) is taken instead of the flask, if but two or three drops of As_2O_3 solution is used and the apparatus held at arm's length, the experiment is a perfectly safe one even in a closed room. This is stated so explicitly because a few teachers are overcautious and omit many experiments, while on the other hand a few are culpably careless.

This last experiment is **Marsh's test** for "arsenic" (any compound of arsenicum). Of course in all tests the chemist must first make sure that his materials are pure, or at least free from the substance he is searching for in the unknown liquid or material. (See MAGNESIUM.)

Arsenicum (and its compounds) is a powerful **antiseptic**. Bodies of those poisoned with it are sometimes pre-

ARSENICUM, ANTIMONY, AND CHROMIUM. 91

served from putrefaction for years. In small doses it stimulates and causes persons to grow fat. It is said to beautify the complexion, but its use is a very dangerous practice. All the symptoms of arsenical poisoning appear, if one ceases the practice. It is a singular fact that in a certain district of Hungary the peasants habitually eat "arsenic."

Antimony (sp. gr. 6.7) is a brittle, highly **crystalline** solid (semi-metal), with brilliant luster. Upon the surface of its bluish-white masses are usually fern-like crystallizations.

EXP. 110.—Into an acidulated (H Cl) dilute solution of antimony (tartar emetic, K Sb O $C_4H_4O_6$, potassium "antimonyl" tartrate) pass H_2S gas (or its solution). Sb_2S_3, antimonous sulphide, *orange-yellow*, falls. Filter, dry, and heat carefully; it turns *grayish-black*.

Native **antimonous sulphide** (gray antimony, or antimony glance) is the source of the Sb of commerce.

EXP. 111.—Perform EXP. 109, using antimonial solution instead of arsenical. Dark antimony spots are obtained. Upon one place solution of calcium chloride, it is *unaffected;* upon another place a drop of hot nitric acid, it is oxidized (turned white, Sb_2O_3), but *not* dissolved. (See Remarks, EXP. 108.)

Antimony is a constituent of several important alloys, as type metal, etc. (See ALLOYS.)

An **alloy** is a mechanical mixture of two or more metals (including semi-metals). If one of the metals is mercury, the alloy is called an **amalgam.** A mechanical mixture differs from a chemical compound in that it may contain its constituents in *any* proportions, but a chemical compound must contain each constituent in some one proportion, or *multiple of that proportion*.

Chromium (sp. gr. 4.8) is a silver-white metal (considered a metal, though ordinarily negative to H). (Let the student learn right here that the order of elements in Table No. 1 is the *usual* order. Rarely an element takes a different position when obtained by electrolysis under different circumstances, or from different compounds.)

Chromium makes both acid-forming (Cr O_3) and basic (Cr_2O_3) oxides with corresponding acid ($H_2Cr\ O_4$ chromic acid) and base ($Cr_2\ 6\ H\ O$) respectively.

The principal ore of chromium is **"chromic iron ore"** (Fe $Cr_2\ O_4$). A few of its compounds are extensively used in the arts, viz.: potassium chromate ($K_2Cr\ O_4$), potassium bichromate (di-) ($K_2Cr_2O_7$), and lead chromate (Pb Cr O_4) "chrome yellow." (See ANA. CHARTS.)

CHAPTER XXVI.

GOLD AND PLATINUM.

NOTE.—With this chapter we begin the study of the metals proper. In general, a **metal** is an elementary substance (1) with a peculiar luster, called metallic, (2) insoluble in water, (3) a good conductor of heat and electricity, (4) positive, with reference to hydrogen, and (5) uniting with H and O to form bases. Chemists are not, however, agreed as to any precise definition, and the line between metals and non-metals cannot be sharply drawn. This is the case with terms used in all sciences (except in the exact sciences, included in the general term mathematics). No line can be drawn between soluble and insoluble substances, for one kind fades gradually into the other. For example, Pb is considered insoluble, but traces of the metal may be found in distilled water that has been in a leaden dish for a day or two. It oxidizes and dissolves. No line can be definitely drawn between "hot" substances and "cold" ones, but the terms are relative. The same is true of poisonous and non-poisonous substances.

In the arts an alloy of two or more metals is often spoken of as "the metal," but this is a technical and loose use of the term.

GOLD AND PLATINUM.   93

For uses of the metals, reduction of their ores, etc., see fuller accounts in the cyclopædia and in larger works on chemistry. See also APPENDIX.

Gold (sp. gr. 19.3, fusing point 1,100°) is found native (free), frequently alloyed with silver, in **quartz** veins, alluvial deposits ("placers"), etc. It is obtained by (1) **quartz mining**, (2) **placer mining**, and (3) **hydraulic mining.**

EXP. 112.—Dissolve a piece of gold-leaf in globule of Hg. Place the amalgam on hard glass and in window with outward draft; keep at dull red heat for a little time. Hg distills leaving the gold.

Mercury is used to extract gold from the sands or from pulverized quartz. The amalgam of Au and Hg is then submitted to pressure in "bags," which squeezes out much of the Hg. The remainder is driven off by distillation, but the Hg is saved, not thrown away as in the experiment.

Gold is a very brilliant orange-yellow solid, the most ductile and malleable of the metals (280,000 sheets of the finest gold-leaf make only one inch in thickness). It was known as the "king of metals," and together with platinum and silver (also rare metals of platinum group) is called a **noble metal.** The others in contrast are called **base metals.** It is insoluble in any of the common acids, but dissolves in **"aqua regia,"** chlorine-water, or bromine-water.

Pure gold is too soft for jewelry, coin, etc., and is hardened by copper. A carat is $\frac{1}{24}$. An alloy containing $\frac{16}{24}$ pure gold is said to be gold of 16 carats fine.

Aurous cyanide (Au C N) dissolved in solution of K C N is used in electro-gilding. The clean substance to be plated is hung upon the negative pole of the battery and gold upon the positive pole.

Platinum (sp. gr. 21.5, fus. pt. 2,000°) is found native, usually alloyed ("platinum ore") with iron, copper, or some of the rare metals (*palladium* used to color "salmon" bronze, *rhodium*, *iridium* used to tip gold pens, *ruthenium* and *osmium*) of the platinum group. Like gold, it is insoluble in any one of the common acids, but dissolves in chlorine-water, and slowly in aqua regia (H Cl + H N O$_3$). Its "ore" is worked by means of the oxy-hydrogen blowpipe, coal gas being usually used in place of H.

Platinum—because of its **high fusing point** and its insolubility in most liquids—is to the chemist an exceedingly useful metal. From it he makes crucibles, stills (see H$_2$S O$_4$), wire, blowpipe tips, etc.

CHAPTER XXVII.

SILVER, MERCURY, AND LEAD.

Silver (sp. gr. 10.5, fus. pt. 1,040°) is found native, often alloyed with copper, mercury, and gold. Ag$_2$S (mixed with other sulphides, as galena, Pb S) and Ag Cl ("**horn silver**") are among its chief ores.

Exp. 113.—Repeat Exp. 6 and place the resulting Ag Cl, mixed with a little K$_2$C O$_3$ (or Na$_2$C O$_3$) upon charcoal and heat in reducing flame of the blowpipe. A silver globule ("button") is obtained.

$$(1) - K_2C O_3 + 2 Ag Cl = Ag_2C O_3 + 2 K Cl \nearrow$$

$$(2) - Ag_2C O_3 = Ag_2O + C O_2 \nearrow$$

$$(3) - 2 Ag_2O + \underset{\substack{\text{deoxidizing} \\ \text{agent}}}{C} = Ag_4 + C O_2 \nearrow$$

SILVER, MERCURY, AND LEAD. 95

The melted globule absorbs oxygen from the air, and if cooled quickly the escaping O breaks the hardening surface, and the melted ("molten") silver runs out ("spitting" or "sprouting").

Silver is a brilliant white metal. For jewelry, coin, etc., it is hardened with Cu. It is used for silvering mirrors because it takes a *high polish*. It is not acted upon by fused caustic alkalies (K H O, Na H O, etc.), as glass and platinum are, and hence certain chemical vessels are made from the metal. It expands at the moment of solidification and hence can be cast (*copies fine lines of the mould*).

Silver is obtained from the sulphide by (1) roasting the pulverized ore with salt, $Ag_2S + 2\,Na\,Cl = 2\,Ag\,Cl + Na_2S$, and (2) by placing the Ag Cl in a cylinder with H_2O, Hg and Fe scraps, $2\,Ag\,Cl + Fe = Fe\,Cl_2 + Ag_2$. The Hg forms an amalgam with silver from which the Ag is obtained, as gold is obtained from gold amalgam. The process of EXP. 113 is too *expensive* for the practical miner, though used by the assayer.

Silver may be freed from lead by fusing the alloy, and as Pb crystallizes first it may be skimmed out. This leaves a portion of the Pb, which may be completely extracted by **cupellation.** (A **cupel** is a shallow dish made of bone ashes.) The Ag containing Pb and other impurities is placed in the cupel and raised to the red heat. A hot current of air plays upon the fused mass. The Pb is oxidized and the Pb O is absorbed by the cupel. After a while the refiner sees the mirror-like globule of pure silver and quickly removes it, lest it also oxidize and waste.

Silver nitrate (Ag N O_3, **lunar caustic**) is the most important salt of silver. It forms with organic compounds by the action of light a very *stable*, dark compound, and hence is used in **indelible inks.** Hair dyes sometimes contain it, but these are highly injurious.

The changes which the salts of silver undergo when exposed to light, especially in presence of organic matter, is the basis of **photography.** (See EXP. 6, NOTE.)

EXP. 114.—Borrow an old "negative" from a photographer, and upon a sheet of prepared paper (moistened with silver salt and dried in the dark) furnished by him, print by means of a few moments' exposure to direct sunlight, a photograph. After removal and a few hours' exposure (even to reflected light), the picture fades out, because the entire paper turns black.

The photographer applies reagents to dissolve from the unblackened portion the silver salt, and thus preserves the picture. In preparing the negative he first covers the glass with an organic film (collodion) to receive the silver salts. (Hold a lens up between the window and a sheet of paper. The lens converges the rays of light and forms an inverted image of the window upon the paper. This explains the formation of the "negative" in the dark "camera.") After the formation of the image, he treats the slide (glass) with reagents whose action upon the part previously influenced by the light is different from their action upon the part uninfluenced by the light. The silver salts upon the unblackened portion are dissolved and the blackened portion is "fixed" so that his picture does not fade out like ours. But the simple principle of photography should be learned here, not the art. (See APPENDIX.)

A solution of Ag C N in solution of K C N is used in electroplating. The clean substance to be plated is hung upon the negative pole, and silver upon the positive.

Mercury or **"quicksilver"** (sp. gr. 13.5, fus. pt., *i. e.*, freezing point—39.4°) is found native in small quantities, but its chief source is the ore **cinnabar** (Hg S mercuric sulphide) from which the liquid metal is obtained by mixing with iron turnings (or lime) and distilling.

$$Hg\,S + Fe = Fe\,S + Hg$$

When Hg S is prepared artificially (by "subliming" together S and Hg) it is called **vermilion** and is used as a pigment.

Mercury is largely used in making thermometers, barometers, etc., for collecting gases soluble in water (see FIG. 24), for extracting gold and silver from their ores, for silvering mirrors (tin amalgam), and formerly was much more used in medicine than now.

SILVER, MERCURY, AND LEAD. 97

"*Blue pill*" is Hg "rubbed up" with confection of roses till the globules are not visible to the naked eye. Blue ointment is mercury "rubbed up" with lard.

Exp. 115.—Pour a little dilute nitric acid upon a considerable quantity of Hg, and, bringing to boiling point, leave over night; pour off from the excess of Hg and preserve as solution of mercuro*us* nitrate ($Hg_2 2 N O_3$). Dissolve a small globule of Hg *completely* in an excess of hot, strong nitric acid. Evaporate nearly to dryness, dilute and preserve as solution of mercur*ic* nitrate ($Hg 2 N O_3$). (Of course these salts may be obtained dry by evaporation over a water-bath.)

Exp. 116.—To a solution of mercurous nitrate add H Cl.

$$Hg_2 2 N O_3 + 2 H Cl = \underset{\substack{\text{white} \\ \text{precipitate}}}{Hg_2 Cl_2} + 2 H N O_3$$

Mercurous chloride (**calomel**, $Hg_2 Cl_2$) is an insoluble (in water) white powder. It acts powerfully upon the glandular system (liver, etc.), and in large or long continued doses produces **salivation** (excessive action of the salivary glands) and other serious results. It was formerly used in medicine much more than now, by some almost as a "cure all."

Exp. 117.—To a solution of mercuric nitrate add H Cl.

$$Hg 2 N O_3 + 2 H Cl = Hg Cl_2 + 2 H N O_3$$

There is no precipitate because $Hg Cl_2$ is soluble. Place *one drop* of the solution on clean glass and evaporate at *low heat*. White crystals of $Hg Cl_2$ are obtained.

Mercuric chloride (Hg Cl_2 **corrosive sublimate**) is a powerful poison and a strong **antiseptic**. It is used to prevent the decay of wood, and its dilute solution in alcohol brushed over specimens in Natural History preserves them. (See ANTIDOTES.)

Lead (sp. gr. 11.4, fus. pt. 334°) is rarely found free. Its chief ore is lead sulphide (Pb S, galena), often carrying Ag_2S. The roasting ("smelting") of this ore and separation of the metal is a very simple process. Pb is soft and malleable, and when fresh cut has a lustrous bluish-gray color, quickly dulled by oxidation. Its common uses are well known to every school-boy. It contracts in solidifying, and hence will not make accurate castings (*i. e.*, will not copy the fine lines of the mould).

EXP. 118.—Make two moulds by boring conical cavities into plaster of Paris ($CaSO_4, 2H_2O$) and making fine, clean-cut grooves on the sides. Into one pour pure melted lead. Into the other pour melted lead, in which a little Sb and Sn has been previously dissolved (type metal). The first casting is blunt and does not copy the grooves; the second is sharp, pointed, and copies the grooves accurately. This is caused by expansion of the *crystalline* Sb and Sn in solidifying. [Sb alone may be used as well.]

Water used for drinking purposes should not be brought great distances in lead pipes (unless the water contains considerable quantities of phosphates, carbonates, or sulphates, which coat the lead with white coat), and water that has stood over night in the short lead pipe connecting with faucet should be allowed to run out before drinking. Water containing even minute quantities (and otherwise practically harmless) of ammoniacal salts (from decomposition of organic matter) dissolves lead and keeps the surface *bright*. Chronic lead poisoning is produced by drinking such water. Lead is an "accumulative" poison, *i. e.*, it remains in the system and is thrown off with difficulty. Painters are often attacked by "colic" produced by lead poisoning.

Fruit cans should not be soldered with an alloy of Pb. (See EXP. 120 and connection.) Metallic Pb is not poisonous because of its insolubility. (Plumbers are not attacked by "lead colic.")

SILVER, MERCURY, AND LEAD. 99

Litharge (Pb O) (see Exp. 50)—"red lead" ($Pb_3 O_4$)—**"sugar of lead"** (lead acetate Pb 2 $C_2 H_3 O_2$). and **"white lead"** chiefly (Pb C O_3 but containing a little Pb 2 H O) used in painting, are important compounds. All are poisonous, especially the very *soluble* acetate. (See ANTIDOTES, also Exp. 12.)

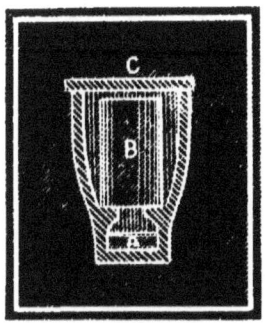

Fig. 37.

White lead is made as represented in Fig. 37. A roll of lead (B) is placed in an earthen vessel, and below, weak vinegar (A). Above (and around) is packed decaying tan-bark (C) and refuse. These vessels are arranged in immense piles; the heat of the decomposition assists the evaporation of the vinegar, and in five or six weeks the lead is all converted into Pb C O_3.

$$Pb + O + H C_2H_3O_2 = Pb H O C_2H_3O_2$$
from air   from vinegar   basic salt

$$C O_2 + Pb H O C_2H_3O_2 = Pb C O_3 + H C_2H_3O_2$$
from decomposing refuse   basic lead acetate (see basic salts)   "white lead"   unites with another portion of Pb

White lead is often largely adulterated with gypsum (Ca S O_4 2 H_2O) heavy spar (Ba S O_4), etc. Pure Pb C O_3 dissolves *completely* in hot dilute H N O_3, and the adulteration is easily detected.

EXP. 119. Add a little mucilage to lead acetate solution (sympathetic ink) and write with fine hand a few words. Dry; they are invisible. Moisten the paper and allow H_2S gas to come in contact with it. The letters become black. (See EXP. 9.)

H_2S is a test for lead, and, *vice versa*, lead acetate (paper moistened with it) is a test for H_2S. "*A body acted upon characteristically by a reagent is as good a test for the reagent as the reagent is for it.*"—*Attfield*. (See test in ANA. CHARTS.)

CHAPTER XXVIII.

Cu, Fe, Zn, and Sn.

Copper (sp. gr. 8.9, fus. pt. 1,200°) is found free in large masses (Lake Superior mines). Its most common ore is copper pyrites ($Fe\,Cu\,S_2$), from which it is obtained by roasting with a silicate, or with silica ($Si\,O_2$), to remove the iron as iron silicate, and again roasting the Cu S. It is a reddish metal, highly malleable and ductile. With the exception of Ag it is the best conductor of heat and electricity. Brass, bronze, and bell-metal contain Cu. (See ALLOYS.)

The salts of copper are poisonous. (See ANTIDOTES.) Substances containing acids (fruits, jellies, pickles, etc.) should never be put in copper (or brass) utensils. Fats dissolve copper oxide, and therefore should be put into copper dishes only when the vessels are bright. Copper sulphate ("blue vitriol," "blue stone" $Cu\,S\,O_4\,5\,H_2O$) is used in calico printing and in galvanic batteries. (See EXP. 34.) The native malachite ($Cu\,C\,O_3 + Cu\,2\,H\,O$) takes a high polish and is used for jewelry and other ornamental articles. Verdigris is copper acetate ($Cu\,2\,C_2\,H_3\,O_2$) though the name is often applied to the artificial carbonate.

Iron (sp. gr. 7.8, fus. pt. 1,000° to 1,800°) is the most important of all the metals. It is rarely found free (always found free in aerolites) but in combination it is widely distributed, traces being found in the blood of animals and in the juices of plants. It is a soft, silver-white metal (if pure). Among the most important of its numerous ores are Fe_2O_3 ("specular iron" hematite)— $Fe_2 6 H O + Fe_2 O_3$ (brown hematite, limonite)— $Fe_3 O_4$ ("magnetic iron"), and $Fe C O_3$ (spathic iron, ferro*us* carbonate). The value of the ore depends as much upon the nature of its impurities as upon the percentage of iron.

The old process of reduction ("Direct Process") was to roast the ore with charcoal in an open "forge" fire. The pasty mass of reduced iron, called "bloom" separates from the fused silicates (or fused glass), called "slag."

The modern process ("Indirect") consists of two parts, (1) obtaining the reduced iron from the ore, not pure, but containing a large percentage of C. (This is cast iron, or **"pig iron."**) (2) The production of iron nearly free from C (**"wrought iron"**) from the cast iron.

1. The ore is placed in a "blast furnace" with layers of coal, coke, and "flux" [the last, limestone $Ca C O_3$, if impurities are silicates (clayey), and silicates, if the impurities are calcareous. Of course, the object is to form a "slag" of calcium glass]. Hot air is driven in below. The heat of the furnace is intense and its action continuous. The "life" of the furnace fire is often twenty years, fresh material being ceaselessly supplied from above. The melted iron and "slag" (floating on iron) is drawn off below. [The hot $C O_2$ and unburnt gases passing from chimney are utilized for heating the air driven in below.] The iron runs into a large main, called "sow," and thence into lateral moulds called "pigs" (hence "pig iron").

2. **Pig iron** (2 to 5 per cent. of C) is changed to wrought iron (less than ½ per cent. of C) by burning out the C (also S, Si, and P) in a reverberatory furnace, "puddling furnace" (Fig. 38). Fuel burns upon the grate A; pig iron is placed upon the floor B, and is frequently stirred by means of openings in the side.

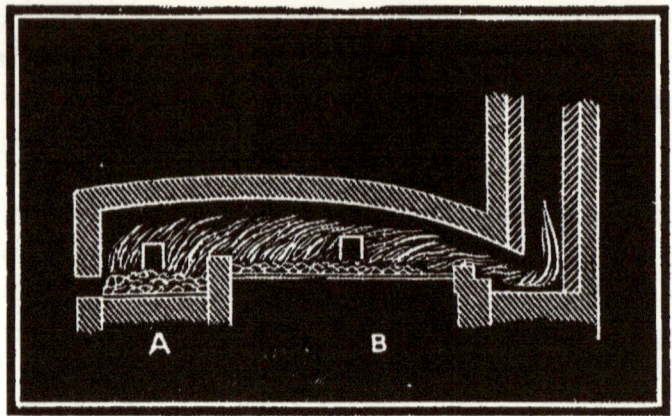

Fig. 38.

Steel contains more C than wrought iron and less than cast iron. It may be made by heating bars of wrought iron to redness in contact with powdered charcoal for eight or ten days. This is called the cementation process.

Bessemer steel is made by decarbonizing the best pig iron (free from phosphorus and sulphur) at a fearful heat in an egg-shaped vessel ("*converter*") lined with infusible material. Hot air is driven in below through numerous openings by means of a powerful engine. Si is also removed. "Looking-glass" iron containing a known quantity of C and a little Mn is then added. Bessemer's process is a rapid one. Bessemer steel is largely used in constructing railroads, bridges, etc.

Steel expands at the moment of solidification and therefore can be cast. Few metals besides iron can be welded. (To be welded a metal must soften before melting.) Cast iron cannot be welded. Iron (or its salts) is largely used in medicine as a tonic.

Ferrous sulphate (Fe S O_4, 7 H_2O, green vitriol, copperas) is used in dyeing, making ink, etc. Fe S is used in preparing the reagent H_2S (Exp. 8). Iron disulphide (Fe S_2, **iron pyrites,** "fool's gold") may be readily distinguished from gold by heating and observing the odor of S O_2 and also the change in color. (See Exp. 91.)

Zinc (sp. gr. 6.9, fus. pt. 410°) very rarely occurs native. Its chief ores are $Zn\,CO_3$ (smithsonite), $Zn\,S$ (zinc blende), and $Zn\,O$ ("red zinc ore" colored red by an oxide of Mn). It is a bluish-white crystalline metal. Fe dipped in melted Zn is coated with the metal and forms what is termed **galvanized iron.** Water that has stood a long time in zinc-lined vessels (tanks) is unfit to drink. $Zn\,O$ (zinc white) is used as paint. (See ALLOYS.)

Tin (sp. gr. 7.3, fus. pt. 230°) is obtained from its principal ore $Sn\,O_2$ (tin dioxide, stann*i*c oxide, **"tin stone"**) by roasting with carbon in reverberatory furnace. It is a lustrous, white, highly *crystalline* metal, malleable and ductile. When a bar of tin is bent, a crackling sound ("*tin cry*"), caused by the friction among the crystals, is heard.

"**Tin ware**" is really iron ware coated with Sn (by dipping the iron into melted tin). When the tin wears off, the iron rust (Fe_2O_3, or hydrated $Fe_2\,6\,H\,O$) is seen. Tin is often adulterated with (the cheaper) lead. Fruit contained in cans coated with such "tin" is unfit to eat, for it contains poisonous lead salts. Solder for such cans should contain no lead. Pb is easily detected by

EXP. 120.—Upon a piece of "tin" (tinned iron) place a drop of $H\,N\,O_3$ and evaporate to dryness. Add a drop of $K\,I$ solution, *yellow* $Pb\,I_2$ is formed if lead is present. [Try the experiment with a piece of "tin" upon which a minute piece of lead has been melted, forming alloy.]

$$Pb\,2\,N\,O_3 + 2\,K\,I = 2\,K\,N\,O_3 + \underset{\text{yellow}}{Pb\,I_2}$$

Pins made of brass wire, copper utensils, iron tacks, etc., are often covered with a thin coat of tin to give bright surface. Tin is largely used in making alloys (which see).

Tin disulphide ($Sn\,S_2$), a bright golden-yellow, is known as **mosaic gold,** and is used in decorative painting. $Sn\,Cl_2$ (stannous chloride) and $Sn\,Cl_4$ (ic) are largely used in dyeing.

CHAPTER XXIX.

Bi, Co, Ni, Mn, Al, and Mg.

Bismuth (sp. gr. 9.8, fus. pt. 264°) is a brittle, purplish-white, crystalline metal. It forms alloys with other metals, expanding much in solidifying and *remarkable for their low melting point.*

EXP. 121.—Fuse Bi (5 deg.), Pb (3 deg.), and Sn (2 deg.) together. The alloy is **fusible metal** (one variety). Place the cold globule in water and raise to the boiling point. Notice that the alloy melts (at 91.6°) before the water boils.

Fusible metal is used for taking casts of wood cuts, etc. Fusible metal (of different composition and melting at some definite point above 100°) is used for "safety plugs" in steam engines. When the temperature approaches a point that would be dangerous, the plugs melt and let the steam escape.

Cobalt (sp. gr. 8.6) is a silver-white metal. Its salts (acetate, sulphate, nitrate, chloride) are used for sympathetic ink. (See cyclopædia.)

EXP. 122.—Thicken a solution of cobalt chloride with a little pure mucilage. Write with a fine pen upon paper. The writing is invisible. Heat upon metallic support. The writing is distinctly *blue*. [Dry $CoCl_2$ is distinctly blue, but moist $CoCl_2$ has a pale pink color and is invisible when thin spread. The salt is deliquescent.] The ink becomes invisible again when the paper cools.

Nickel (sp. gr. 8.9) is a lustrous white metal, taking a high polish. It is used for plating iron to protect from rusting. It is largely used in alloys.

EXP. 123.—Repeat EXP. 122, using cobalt solution, to which nickel chloride has been added. The writing is *green*. [Nickel salts are used to make *green* sympathetic ink.]

Manganese (sp. gr. 8, fus. pt. about 1,800°) is a hard, brittle metal. It easily oxidizes in the air and hence is not found free. It is best kept under petroleum.

Manganese dioxide ($Mn\ O_2$, see preparation of O and Cl) is its most important ore. **Manganates** (dyad grouping $Mn\ O_4$) and **permanganates** (dyad grouping $Mn_2\ O_8$) are largely used as **disinfectants**.

EXP. 124.—Place a *small* piece of fresh meat in a test-tube of water and leave till putrefaction begins. Filter (through paper) and let fall into it a single drop of *dilute* potassium permanganate ($K_2\ Mn_2\ O_8$). Place beside it a second test-tube of distilled water in which the *same amount* of permanganate has been put. Leave both over night. The permanganate in the first test-tube is decolorized, having given up a part of its O to the decomposed organic matter. In the second the color remains. [The presence of ferrous salts, or other easily oxidizable substances, must be avoided. Water through which the breath has been blown by means of a glass tube answers for the test.]

Potassium permanganate is a powerful **oxidizing agent** and is a very delicate test for the presence of decomposing organic matter. [In such tests be careful not to add too much $K_2\ Mn_2\ O_8$, as of course the excess would not be decolorized.]

Aluminum (or aluminium, sp. gr. 2.6, fus. pt. 700°) is a bluish-white metal, taking a bright polish. Next to silicon and oxygen it is the most abundant element in the earth's crust. It does not readily oxidize in the air. Delicate, light weights, and, in general, instruments needing lightness and moderate strength are made from aluminum.

Aluminum bronze (Cu 90 per cent., Al 10 per cent.) is a very hard alloy, malleable, has the color of gold, and takes a fine polish.

Aluminum oxide (Al_2O_3) occurs in corundum, ruby, sapphire, and emery (impure).

Common **clay** is chiefly aluminum silicate, $Al_2Si_2O_7$ (there are numerous silicate "groupings"), but *no cheap method* of obtaining the metal has yet been discovered. Al would be extensively used were it not for its high price. (See GLASS and PORCELAIN.)

Common **alum** is a double sulphate (Al_2K_2 4 S O_4, 24 H_2O) containing much water of crystallization. Ammonium alum [$Al_2(H_4N)_2$ 4 S O_4, 24 H_2O] is also somewhat common. Alum is much used as a "mordant" in dyeing. (See DYEING.) Cryolite is $Al_2F_6 + 6$ Na F.

Magnesium (sp. gr. 1.75, fus. pt. about 2,000°, but igniting point is low, the flame of a candle being sufficient to set it on fire) is a silver-white metal not found native, but in combination is widely distributed. Mg burns in the air with a brilliant light (EXP. 3), forming Mg O ("magnesia"). [In general, the ending *a* means (1) the oxide, (2) the carbonate, or (3) the hydrate of the metal.]

The light from burning Mg is rich in chemical (actinic) rays, and hence is used for photographing in dark caves, etc. Arsenicum is never found with it, and the metal is used instead of Zn in important tests for As. (See Marsh's test.)

Mg Cl_2 is found in sea water. Mg S O_4, 7 H_2O (Epsom salt) is found in many mineral waters and in sea water. "Magnesia alba" is an artificial mixture of Mg C O_3 and Mg 2 H O, principally the former. (See magnesite, hornblende, meerschaum, soapstone, talc, serpentine, dolomite, etc., in cyclopædia.)

CHAPTER XXX.

CALCIUM, STRONTIUM, AND BARIUM.

Calcium (sp. gr. 1.58) is a light-yellow, ductile metal. It oxidizes in moist air and consequently is not found native (free). Its compounds are widely diffused.

Calcium oxide (Ca O, **quicklime,** a basic oxide, EXP. 5) is prepared by heating the native carbonate (Ca C O_3) in egg-shaped "kilns" till C O_2 is all expelled. A kiln in which the process is continuous is shown in Fig. 39.

Reaction: Ca C O_3 = Ca O + C O_2

Mixed with sand, hair, etc., according to the purpose for which it is intended, calcium oxide is used for making mortar, cements, etc.

The principal reactions are:—

(1)—Ca O + H_2O   Ca 2 H O
                             "water-slacked lime"

When exposed to the air, this absorbs C O_2 and hardens.

(2)—Ca 2 H O + C O_2 Ca C O_3 + H_2O
    "water slacked   from   "air-slacked   evaporates
     lime"   air   lime"

Hydraulic mortars possess the power of hardening under water. These are made from quicklime that has been prepared from calcium carbonate containing a large percentage of silicates. *Roman cement* is made from calcium oxide containing from 25 to 35 per cent. of clay and hardens under water in a few hours. Chalk and clay thoroughly ground together with water, dried, and carefully burnt in kilns, produce an impure quicklime from which a good hydraulic mortar, called *Portland cement*, is made. The hardening of these mortars, like those above, depends upon the formation of calcium carbonate.

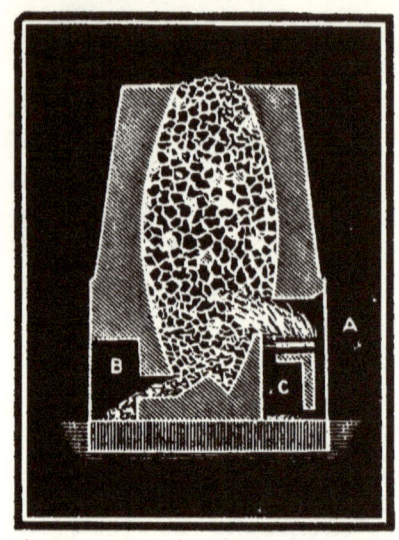

Fig. 39. A—fire. C—ash-pit. Calcium carbonate is put in at top of furnace and calcium oxide removed at B.

Ca O falls to a powder when gradually air-slacked by exposure. It first absorbs water and then CO_2 as in above reactions.

Ca O is used in the laboratory for drying gases (EXPS. 45, 56, and illuminating gas) and in the "lime light" (see APPENDIX), the flame of the oxy-hydrogen blowpipe raising it to the *white heat* and causing it to emit an intense light.

Calcium carbonate ($CaCO_3$) is found as marble, limestone, shells (chalk is formed by beds of tiny shells), stalactites, etc., also with $Ca_3 2 PO_4$ in bones. (See HARD WATER and EXP. 51.)

Calcium sulphate ($CaSO_4$, anhydrite) and calcium sulphate *with water of crystallization* ($CaSO_4, 2H_2O$ **gypsum,** plaster, alabaster) occur native. When heated to 120°, gypsum parts with its water of crystallization, forming **"plaster of Paris."** This plaster soon hardens ("sets") when mixed with water and hence is used as cement, and for taking casts. (See WATER permanently hard.)

CALCIUM, STRONTIUM, AND BARIUM. 109

Calcium chloride ($Ca Cl_2$) has so strong an attraction for water that it is deliquescent. It is used for drying gases and is a constituent of bleaching powder (which see).

Calcium fluoride ($Ca F_2$, fluor spar) occurs native and is used as a flux in the reduction of metals. The peculiar glowing of this mineral when heated gave rise to the term fluorescence. Hydrofluoric acid is prepared from this salt by the action of sulphuric acid. (See EXP. 86.)

Barium (sp. gr. 4) and **Strontium** (sp. gr. 2.5) resemble calcium.

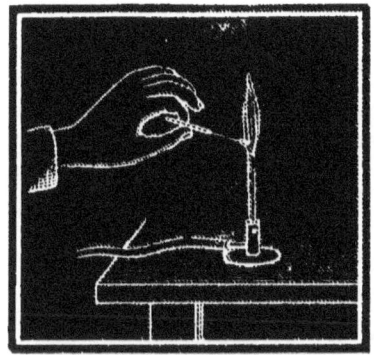

Fig. 40.

EXP. 125.—Dissolve a barium salt in a little dilute H Cl. Make a loop upon one end of a short platinum wire and fuse upon the other end a piece of glass tubing for a handle. Introduce into the lower and outer flame of Bunsen's burner (Fig. 40) by means of this loop a little of Ba salt solution. The flame is colored *green*. [$Ba Cl_2$ dissolved in water answers.]

Barium salts (especially $Ba 2 N O_3$) are used to give the color in **green** fire (in pyrotechny) and this color is a very good test for soluble or volatilizable salts of Ba.

Barium sulphate ($Ba S O_4$, heavy spar) is often used to adulterate white lead ($Pb C O_3$). Barium chloride ($Ba Cl_2$) is test for soluble sulphates. (EXP. 94.)

EXP. 126.—Repeat EXP. 125, using Sr salt instead of Ba salt. The flame is colored *red*.

Strontium salts are used to give the color in **red** fire, and this color is a very good test for soluble or volatilizable salts of Sr.

CHAPTER XXXI.

POTASSIUM, SODIUM, AMMONIUM.

Potassium (sp. gr. .87, fus. pt. 63°) is a light, bluish-white metal, soft enough (at 15°) to be spread with a knife.

Fig. 41.

EXP. 127.—Cut a small slice of K upon blotting paper. Trim away the edges and throw the cleaned piece upon water in a beaker. Cover with glass plate (impurities cause spattering). The K decomposes the water.

$$K + H_2O = KHO + H$$

The reaction is so violent that the liberated hydrogen takes fire, and in burning the heat volatilizes a little of the K, which in burning colors the flame *purple*.

The affinity of potassium for O is so great that it must be kept under naptha ($C_{10}H_{16}$ containing no O). EXP. 127 proves that it cannot be found free or native.

The compounds of K are widely distributed. They are constituents of all plants and of the bodies of animals. Potassium hydrate (K H O "**caustic potash**") is a *white solid* made from K_2CO_3 by action of Ca 2 H O (and heat).

$$K_2CO_3 + Ca\,2\,H\,O = 2\,KHO + CaCO_3$$

It is largely used in the manufacture of soap. It is one of the strongest alkalies known. (See SOAP and ANTIDOTES.)

Potassium carbonate ($K_2 C O_3$ "**pearlash**") is prepared by leaching wood ashes, evaporating the "**lye**" in large pots (hence potash), and purifying by crystallization. It is a deliquescent salt, with a strong alkaline reaction. It (or $Na_2 C O_3$) is largely used in chemical analysis. [See ANA. CHARTS, silver, lead, etc.] It reacts with insoluble silicates by change of partners.

$$\begin{array}{c}\text{The metallic}\\ \text{silicate}\\ \text{(insoluble)}\end{array} + \begin{array}{c}\text{potassium}\\ \text{carbonate}\end{array} = \begin{array}{c}\text{potassium}\\ \text{silicate}\end{array} + \begin{array}{c}\text{the metallic}\\ \text{carbonate}\\ \text{(soluble)}\end{array}$$

"**Saleratus**" ($H K C O_3$ **bicarbonate of potash**, acid salt with alkaline reaction, see ACID-SALTS) may be prepared by passing $C O_2$ through strong solution of the normal salt ($K_2 C O_3$).

$$H_2 O + C O_2 = H_2 C O_3$$
$$K_2 C O_3 + H_2 C O_3 = 2 H K C O_3$$

Potassium nitrate ($K N O_3$ **saltpetre, nitre**) together with $Ca 2 N O_3$ and $Na N O_3$, is formed by the decomposition of refuse organic matter. The white incrustation often seen about such matter is principally $K N O_3$. It is a strong **antiseptic**, and is used with $Na Cl$ (common salt) for preserving meat. It is largely used in the manufacture of gunpowder. When gunpowder burns, the reaction may be represented thus:—

$$\underset{\substack{\text{solid}\\\text{oxidizing}\\\text{age t}}}{2 K N O_3} + \underset{\substack{\text{solid}\\\text{combustible}\\\text{substance}}}{S} + \underset{\substack{\text{solid}\\\text{combustible}\\\text{substance}}}{C_3} = \underset{\substack{\text{gas at}\\\text{temperature}\\\text{of explosion}}}{K_2 S} + \underset{gas}{N_2} + \underset{gas}{3 C O_2}$$

Fireworks are composed of gunpowder containing an excess of C and S with coloring matter.

Potassium chlorate ($K Cl O_3$) is largely used for making oxygen and as an oxidizing agent. (EXP. 19, 79, 98, and MATCHES.) It is much used in medicine to allay inflammation of the throat (as gargle), etc. $K_2 Cr_2 O_7$ forms chrome yellow with lead salts. (ANA. CHARTS.)

The intensely poisonous $K C N$ (solution) dissolves gold and silver cyanides for electroplating.

K Cl resembles Na Cl. Potassium salts are largely used in medicine.

Exp. 128.—Repeat Exp. 125, using potassium salt instead of barium salt. The flame is colored *purplish*.

This is a fair test for potassium compounds. Careful flame tests are of great value to the experienced chemist. (See SPECTROSCOPE.)

Sodium (sp. gr. .97) is a light, silver-white, soft metal, resembling potassium. It is used as a reducing agent in preparing silicon, boron, magnesium, and aluminum.

Exp. 129.—Place a small clean piece of Na on water and quickly press below mouth of inverted test-tube by means of wire gauze attached to wooden rod. The water is decomposed and the H, set free, collects in test-tube. (If Na is thrown on hot water the liberated H immediately takes fire.)

Fig. 42.—Decomposing Water by Sodium.

$$Na + H_2O = NaHO + H$$

The above experiment proves that sodium cannot be found free. Like potassium, it must be kept under naptha.

Exp. 130.—Repeat Exp. 125, using sodium salt instead of barium salt. The flame is colored *yellow*.

Sodium chloride (Na Cl, common salt) is the most abundant of the sodium compounds. It is the source from which most compounds and sodium itself are obtained. Its distribution in larger or smaller quantities is almost universal, traces which the spectroscope reveals being found in the atmosphere. It is obtained from immense

POTASSIUM, SODIUM, AMMONIUM. 113

deposits or beds, from saline springs and sea-water (by evaporation). It crystallizes in cubes. (See CRYSTAL-LIZATION.) It is one of our most common **antiseptics.**

Sodium sulphate ($Na_2 S O_4$ $10 H_2 O$, Glauber's salts) is remarkably efflorescent.

Sodium carbonate ($Na_2 C O_3$ $10 H_2 O$, sal soda) is extensively used in the arts. It is made by **Leblanc's process:—**

(1) Common salt and sulphuric acid are heated.

$$2 Na Cl + H_2 S O_4 = Na_2 S O_4 + 2 H Cl$$

The hydrochloric acid is saved by being absorbed (see EXP. 75, and comments) in tower of coke wet with constantly falling water.

(2) The $Na_2 S O_4$ is heated with $Ca C O_3$ (equal wt.) and C (half its wt.) in a reverberatory furnace.

(a)—$Na_2 S O_4$ + C_2 (reducing agent) = $Na_2 S$ + $2 C O_2$

(b)—$Na_2 S$ + $Ca C O_3$ = $\underbrace{Na_2 C O_3 + Ca S}_{\text{"black ash"}}$ (insoluble)

The $Na_2 C O_3$ is then washed out (**lixiviated**) from the "black ash" and purified by **crystallization** (one of the most valuable known means of purifying crystallizable solids).

Acid sodium carbonate ($H Na C O_3$, bicarbonate of soda, **"soda"** of cook-room, see ACID-SALTS) has alkaline reaction, and is prepared by passing $C O_2$ into the normal salt (see $H K C O_3$).

Sodium hydrate ($Na H O$, caustic soda) is made from sodium carbonate (just as $K H O$ from $K_2 C O_3$) and is used in the manufacture of hard soap.

Sodium nitrate ($Na N O_3$, Chilian saltpeter) is a deliquescent salt.

8

Ammonium (H_4N, a hypothetical metal), as we have seen, is a compound radical, closely allied to K and Na. Though it has never been isolated, an alloy of ammonium and mercury (*i. e.*, an amalgam) has been formed.

Ammonium chloride (H_4N Cl, sal ammoniac) is used in medicine, in dyeing, in soldering, and in the laboratory as a reagent and source of ammonia (H_3 N, see EXP. 45).

Ammonium nitrate (EXP. 36) and ammonium carbonate (see ANTIDOTES) are important salts.

Microcosmic salt (H Na H_4N P O_4 + 4 H_2O, see DOUBLE SALTS) is largely used in blowpipe analysis as a flux.

Ammonia hydrate (H_4N H O "ammonia water") is a very strong base and is extensively used (dilute) as a cleansing agent. (See CHEMISTRY OF CLEANING.)

CHAPTER XXXII.

ORGANIC CHEMISTRY.

STARCH, SUGAR, ETC.

Organic chemistry treats of those compounds (composed principally of C, H, N, and O, but all containing C and H) which are formed chiefly by animals or plants in their processes of growth or *partial* decay. No line can be sharply drawn between organic compounds and inorganic. Many compounds which formerly were supposed to be produced only by the "vital force" of the plant or animal, have been formed recently in the laboratory.

STARCH. 115

NOTE.—It is important to remember that we may make two great divisions of "organic substances":—

I. That which is the essential physical basis of life (*bioplasm*).

II. That which is essential only in a secondary sense and is used by the first in accomplishing its work somewhat as an engine uses fuel, water, and the iron rails.

To this second division belong crystalline substances, fats, gelatine, cellulose, etc. Between the inorganic and this first division of the organic, a distinct line can be drawn. This line bounds all possibilities of the laboratory. It is probably within the province of chemistry to produce, unaided by the "vital force," all substances in this second division. The organic cell proper, with its subtle bioplasm, chemists can never hope to form. For example, the chemist's kernel of wheat will never grow. (See SPONTANEOUS GENERATION in cyclopædia.)

As a rule, inorganic substances have few atoms in the molecule, while molecules of organic substances frequently contain a very large number of atoms. Often *different* organic substances contain the same elements in the same proportion. This peculiar relation is called *isomerism*.

EXAMPLE.

Butyric acid and ethyl acetate, two well-known compounds, differing in essential properties, are isomeric, having the "empirical formula" (expressing only the proportions of the elements): $C_4H_8O_2$, but the "rational formula" (which attempts to represent *in some way* the *arrangement* of the atoms in the molecule) of

Butyric acid $= H\ C_4H_7O_2$. (REF. TABLE No. 2, Continued.)
Ethyl acetate $= C_2H_5C_2H_3O_2$. (REF. TABLE No. 2.)

Plants in general prepare food for animals from the mineral kingdom, and animals, after using it, return it to the mineral kingdom again. The organic by *complete* decay returns to the inorganic. The sun's light and heat (EXP. 58) is the motive power by which the plant is enabled to build up the organic out of the inorganic.

Starch ($C_6H_{10}O_5$) is a substance found in all cereals, in many roots, stems, and fruits. It is composed of grains, which the microscope reveals *differing in size and shape in different plants*. These grains swell up and burst on

CHEMICAL PRIMER.

heating with water. Its use for food, in the laundry, etc., is well known. Arrow-root and tapioca are varieties of starch from roots of tropical plants. Sago is starch from the pith of the sago-palm.

The test of starch is iodine, with which it forms a blue compound. (EXP. 84.)

EXP. 131.—Scrape some potato into cold water and squeeze through a linen cloth several times. The insoluble starch remains suspended in the filtrate, while the woody fiber (cellulose) remains upon the filter. After subsidence, pour off the water, and dry. This illustrates the method of obtaining starch from the potato.

When starch is heated to about 205°, it changes into an isomeric compound, **dextrin**, much used instead of gum arabic in making adhesive stamps. Dextrin is also formed if starch is boiled with water slightly acidulated with sulphuric acid. If the boiling is continued longer, the dextrin is converted into starch-sugar ($C_6H_{12}O_6$). Dextrin gives no blue color with iodine.

Gum arabic ($C_{12}H_{22}O_{11}$) exudes from a species of acacia. **Pectose** is a gummy substance found in many fruits and vegetables.

Cellulose ($C_{18}H_{30}O_{15}$), or woody fiber, is the frame-work of the cells of plants, and is found in every part, even in the pulpy fruits. **Linen**, made from the inner bark of flax, and **cotton**—the hollow white hairs around the seed of the cotton plant—are nearly pure cellulose. (See cyclopædia.) If paper is dipped in dilute sulphuric acid (2 vols. H_2SO_4, 1 vol. H_2O) for a few moments, tough **parchment paper** results.

Gun-cotton is cellulose, in which part of the H has been replaced by the negative radical NO_2, by dipping in a mixture of HNO_3 and H_2SO_4. It is very explosive.

Gun-cotton, dissolved in ether (ethyl oxide) and alcohol (ethyl hydrate) forms **collodion,** much used by photographers.

Celluloid is made chiefly from gun-cotton and camphor, by submitting to great pressure. It can be colored in imitation of coral, made into collars and cuffs, and substituted, in general, for ivory. Its manufacture is comparatively a new industry.

Cane-sugar, sucrose ($C_{12}H_{22}O_{11}$), may be obtained from the sugar-cane, beet-root, maple, and certain kinds of

STARCH. 117

palm. In making it from the sugar-cane (1) the canes are crushed, (2) lime (Ca O) is added to the juice to neutralize any acid formed by fermentation, (3) the liquid is evaporated to thick syrup, (4) set aside to cool, (5) the sugar crystallizes, forming brown sugar, (6) it is put into perforated casks to drain. The drainings ("mother liquor") are molasses.

In the process of refining, brown sugar is (1) dissolved, (2) pumped to upper story of the high building, (3) filtered through twilled cotton bags, kept in bath of steam, (4)filtered through animal charcoal (EXP. 48), (5) evaporated in "vacuum pans" (kettles from which air and steam are partially removed by pump, so that the syrup boils at a lower temperature and does not burn), and (6) set aside to crystallize. If in moulds, loaf-sugar results; if in centrifugal machines, granulated. The drainings are syrup or sugar-house molasses.

Caramel is sugar carefully "burnt" so that it loses part, but not all, of its elements of water. It is used for coloring liquors, flavoring confectioneries, etc.

Cane-sugar is not found in animal tissues or secretions, but is changed in the alimentary canal before absorption into grape sugar. [*Medical students should master all the tests for grape sugar in the* APPENDIX.]

Grape-sugar ($C_6H_{12}O_6$). **glucose** (dextrose, starch-sugar, fruit-sugar), is found in honey, figs, grapes, and many kinds of fruit. It has much less sweetening power than cane-sugar.

EXP. 132.—To a solution of grape-sugar (made by boiling a few raisins in water and filtering) add three drops of copper sulphate (5 per cent. solution and slightly acidulated with acetic acid), then add strong solution of K H O (potash or Na H O, soda) till the light blue color of liquid becomes darker. Raise to the boiling point, but do not boil beyond a few seconds. A *yellowish-red* precipitate of *cuprous oxide* (Cu_2O) falls. This is a delicate test for sugar in animal secretions (grape-sugar, or milk-sugar isomeric with cane). (See ADD. EXP.)

Exp. 133.—Divide a solution of cane-sugar into two parts; apply test as in Exp. 132, no cuprous oxide falls. Slightly acidulate the second portion with H_2SO_4, and boil to syrup. The cane-sugar changes to grape-sugar. Dilute and apply test. Yellowish-red Cu_2O falls.—Boil for some time a *minute* quantity of starch in dilute (2 per cent.) sulphuric acid. The starch changes to grape-sugar. Divide into two portions and test the first by iodine; no starch is found. Test the second; grape-sugar is found. Boil cellulose (woody fiber free from *pitch*) in dilute H_2SO_4 and grape-sugar is found in the solution.

The insoluble starch laid up in the seeds of plants is converted into (soluble) sugar by the action of a nitrogenous substance, called *diastase*, in the presence of *warmth* and *moisture*. The sugar is then absorbed by the growing plantlet, and is built into its structure as woody fiber, etc.

Fermentation is a species of decay. A necessary condition is the presence of some nitrogenous ("albuminous") substance, called a ferment, and the growth therein of a fungus plant called *yeast*. This plant is of a low order, and spreads by the rapid multiplication of cells throughout the whole fermenting substance, if it has the needed *warmth* (about 30°) and *moisture*. In the fermentation of substances containing grape-sugar (or cane-sugar, which changes to grape-sugar), there are two stages:—

1. **The Alcoholic Fermentation,** in which the sugar breaks up into *alcohol* and *carbon dioxide*.

$$\underset{\text{grape-sugar}}{C_6H_{12}O_6} = \underset{\text{alcohol}}{2\,C_2H_5HO} + \underset{\text{carbon dioxide}}{2\,CO_2}$$

2. **The Acetic Fermentation,** in which, by exposure to the air, the alcohol is oxidized, forming *acetic acid* and *water*.

$$\underset{\text{ethyl hydrate}}{C_2H_5HO} + \underset{\text{from the air}}{O_2} = \underset{\text{acetate acid}}{HC_2H_3O_2} + \underset{\text{water}}{H_2O}$$

ALCOHOL, ETC.

NOTE.—The two reactions above explain thoroughly the principal results of fermentation. It is evident that the second stage can be prevented, if the air (oxygen) be excluded from the fermenting material. The first stage cannot be prevented "by bottling," provided there is in the substance sufficient nitrogenous material (ferment), and provided the *yeast spores have not been killed* by boiling or by an antiseptic. The second stage follows the first very rapidly, if the temperature is raised (to about 38°, or 100° F). This explains the rapid "souring" of substances in hot weather. The fermentation ("working") in preserves may be checked by boiling and then excluding the air, *thus shutting out the yeast spores.*

Beer, ale, etc., are made from **malt** (grain that has germinated sufficiently to change nearly all the starch to sugar, and in which the fermentation has been checked by drying). The malt is crushed, water added, and heat applied to turn starch to sugar. It is then cooled, hops and yeast are added, when the alcoholic fermentation at once commences.

Wine is made by the fermentation of grape juice. If all the sugar is converted into alcohol and CO_2, **dry wine** results. If the fermentation ceases (from an excess of sugar over the ferment) when only part of the sugar is changed. **sweet wine** results. **Effervescing wine** is sealed in strong bottles while the alcoholic fermentation is going on. In *sour wine* the acetic stage has somewhat progressed.

When any fermented liquor is distilled, the **alcohol** (having a lower boiling point than water) first passes over through the condenser (Fig. 19), together with certain flavoring substances and a certain part of the water. *Brandy* is made by distillation from wine; *rum* from fermented cane-juice; *whisky* from fermented corn, rye, or potatoes; *gin* from fermented barley and rye, and afterwards distilled with juniper-berries (flavoring).

Alcohol ($C_2 H_5 H O$ ethyl hydrate) is the *intoxicating principle* of all varieties of (unadulterated) "liquors." It is a colorless, volatile, inflammable, *poisonous* liquid. Its flame, as we have noticed, is hot and smokeless. It is a valuable *solvent*. Many substances, as resins, etc., insoluble in water, are soluble in alcohol. A solution of a substance (medicinal) in alcohol is a **tincture.** (See VOLATILE OILS.) Strong alcohol contains about 10 per cent.

water, all of which cannot be removed by distillation. It may be removed by Ca O, or some other substance which has a great affinity for water, when anhydrous, or **absolute alcohol,** remains. Anhydrous (white) Cu S O$_4$ (Exp. 34) is test for absolute alcohol. If water is present, the sulphate turns blue. Common alcohol belongs to marsh gas series. Strong alcohol is an *antiseptic.*

Common Ether $(C_2H_5)_2O$, ethyl oxide, is made by distilling alcohol in presence of sulphuric acid. It is a very volatile, inflammable liquid. It produces great "cold" by its evaporation. If blown in a fine spray (from atomizer) upon some part of the body, the rapid cooling produces local anæsthesia by "freezing" (chilling) the spot. It is inhaled as an **anæsthetic,** and is a valuable *solvent.*

There is a large number of alcohols (hydrates of positive radicals) and corresponding ethers (oxides) arranged in series. **Methyl alcohol** (C H$_3$ H O, wood spirit) is formed by the destructive distillation of wood, and resembles ethyl or common alcohol in many particulars. **Amyl alcohol** (C$_5$ H$_{11}$ H O, **fusel oil**) has a very fetid odor, and is much more poisonous than C$_2$H$_5$ H O. It is formed in small quantities in the fermentation of potatoes and grain. Its boiling point is 137°, while that of ethyl alcohol is only 78°. The common alcohol is separated from it by *fractional distillation,* a valuable method of separating liquids whose boiling points differ materially.

The salts of the positive groupings of the ethers, or alcohols, are often termed **"compound ethers"** (Ex.: ethyl nitrate, $C_2H_5N O_3$, etc.). Many of these "compound ethers" are sold as "essences," and they very closely imitate the true essences. Ethyl butyrate ($C_2H_5C_4H_7O_2$) is sold as "essence of pine-apple."

Chloroform (C H Cl$_3$) is made by distilling alcohol with "chloride of lime." It is a colorless, volatile liquid, used as an **anæsthetic** and as a *solvent.*

ALCOHOL, ETC.

Chloral ($C_2H\ Cl_3\ O$), a colorless, oily liquid, is made by passing dry chlorine into alcohol. It combines with water of crystallization, forming a white crystalline substance, the so-called chloral **hydrate** ($C_2H\ Cl_3\ O\ H_2\ O$). Chloral, when taken, reacts with the alkali of the blood, producing chloroform and *inducing sleep*. It is much used in medicine.

Acetic acid ($H\ C_2H_3O_2$, the acid of vinegar), as we have seen, is produced by the fermentation, under the proper conditions, of substances containing sugar. It is produced *in the second stage* by the oxidation of alcohol. Strong acetic acid crystallizes at 17° and is called glacial. The "mother" of vinegar is a fungus plant; it assists the fermentation by absorbing O from the air and giving it up to oxidize the alcohol. When the alcohol is all gone, however, it works mischief. The vinegar itself is oxidized and destroyed (destructive fermentation). Sulphuric acid and pungent spices are often added to vinegar to increase its strength. One gallon of sulphuric acid in a thousand gallons of vinegar is used to prevent the destructive fermentation. A large quantity of $H_2S\ O_4$, however—such as is added by some unscrupulous dealers to make weak vinegar strong—is exceedingly injurious.

Carbolic acid ($C_6H_5H\ O$, phenyl hydrate), better classed with the alcohols (of phenyl series), is obtained from coal-tar. It is a very *poisonous* liquid (it may be obtained crystallized) and is a powerful **antiseptic** and *disinfectant*. Carbolic acid is sometimes confounded with creosote ($C_8H_{10}O_2$), the antiseptic principle of smoke (by which "bacon," etc., is "cured"); indeed, impure carbolic acid is commonly called creosote. (See ANTIDOTES.)

Benzol (C_6H_5H, phenyl hydride—see ILLUMINATING GAS) is a very volatile, inflammable liquid, is a valuable *solvent*, and is used to remove grease spots from silk and woolen articles. From it, by the action of nitric acid, **nitrobenzol** ($C_6H_5N\ O_2$), an oily liquid is prepared. By the action of reducing agents upon nitrobenzol the celebrated **aniline** (C_6H_7N), the source of the "coal-tar" dyes, is prepared. (See DYEING.)

(For tar, coal-tar, naphtha, benzine, kerosene oil, dead-oil, petroleum, bitumen, etc., see cyclopædia.)

There are three great classes of (*organic*) foods:—
1. **Starch,** sugar, and allied bodies.
2. **Oleaginous** substances. (See CHAP. XXXIV.)
3. **Albuminous** substances ("nutritious matter," nitrogenous matter).

Albumen (formula very complex, composed of C, H, N, S, and O) is found nearly pure in white of eggs. Albuminous matter possesses the power of (1) becoming a ferment, (2) of coagulation, and (3) of putrefaction. **Casein** is found in milk, and is coagulated by rennet (acid); **gluten,** in flour, meal, etc.; **fibrin,** in blood, and another variety of fibrin in muscular tissue. (Medical students see ADD. EXP. for *tests*.)

EXP. 134.—Soak a small, clean bone over night in H Cl (30 per cent.). The mineral matters are dissolved, and the soft animal matter left. Wash thoroughly in water and leave in water over night again. Boil the animal matter for some time in a small quantity of water and set aside to cool. A gelatinous substance remains.

Gelatin (formula complex; a nitrogenous substance not belonging to albuminous matter *proper*) is formed by the action of hot water upon animal membranes, tendons, and bones. **Glue** is very impure gelatin. **Isinglass** is a very pure gelatin from the air-bladders of fish. (The mineral, mica, used in the doors and sides of parlor stoves, is often improperly called *isinglass*.)

CHEMISTRY OF COOKING.

Flour consists of gluten, starch, and a little dextrin and sugar. The oily and mineral substances are contained chiefly in the bran of grain, hence "coarse food," as corn meal, graham flour, oatmeal, cracked wheat, etc., are very necessary for the proper development of bone and sinew.

In bread-making the flour, mixed with milk (or water) containing yeast, is set in a warm place, and immediately the alcoholic fermentation begins. The carbon dioxide set free is held by the gluten, causing the dough "to rise." This is kneaded, to distribute evenly the fermentation and to break up the large bubbles of CO_2.

CHEMISTRY OF COOKING. 123

In baking, the CO_2 and alcohol escape. If the oven is too hot, a crust forms too quickly, prevents the escape of the CO_2, and large cavities are formed. If the fire is not hot enough, the CO_2 escapes before the cells are sufficiently hardened, and the bread falls. Sour bread is formed when, before (or while) baking, the second stage (acetic) of fermentation is reached. The acetic stage follows the alcoholic very rapidly if the temperature of fermentation is high. (See NOTES under FERMENTATION.) A *very* slow fire in baking may produce the same result. **Saleratus** ($HKCO_3$, or **soda** $HNaCO_3$, acid salts, but these have alkaline reaction), is added to neutralize any acid that may be formed by this second fermentation.

In raising biscuit, "soda" and "cream of tartar" ($HKC_4H_4O_6$) are used to furnish the CO_2, while the salt that remains is a harmless one.

Common **baking powder** is merely "cream of tartar" and "soda," but it is often adulterated with alum, to make inferior flour look white. Bread containing alum is highly injurious, producing chronic constipation. (See test, ADD. EXP.)

"**Yeast cakes**" are made by exposing *moistened* corn meal (or other similar substance) containing a ferment, to *moderate temperature* till the gluten is in the midst of the alcohol fermentation. The fermentation is then checked by drying. The yeast plant (fungus) throughout the cake may be likened to so much dry *seed*, which needs only to be sown in the right soil (in the dough).

The chemical changes in the body (Physiological Chemistry) are too difficult for insertion in a primary work.

CHAPTER XXXIII.

VEGETABLE ACIDS AND BASES (ALKALOIDS).

Compounds of **oxalic acid** ($H_2C_2O_4$ 2 H_2O), especially $K_2C_2O_4$, and Ca C_2O_4 are found in *rhubarb, sorrel,* etc. (also a very little of the free acid). The acid is a powerful *poison.* It is sold as "salts of lemon" (a *dangerous name*), to remove ink stains. It used to be very expensive, but it is now made on a large scale by heating sawdust and caustic potash (K H O). (See ANTIDOTES and CHEMISTRY OF CLEANING.)

Salts of **tartaric acid** ($H_2C_4H_4O_6$), also minute quantities of the free acid, exist in many fruits, and especially in the *grape* (as acid potassium tartrate, H K $C_4H_4O_6$, see ACID-SALTS). It settles during fermentation, forming a crust ("argol," "bitartrate of potash") which, when purified, is **cream of tartar** (H K C_4 H_4 O_6). **Tartar emetic** is a double *salt: potassium* antimonyl tartrate (K $\overline{Sb\ O\ C_4 H_4 O_6}$). **Rochelle salt** is K Na $C_4 H_4 O_6$.

Citric acid ($H_3C_6H_5O_7H_2O$) is the acid of the lemon, lime, etc. Its salts are also present.

Malic acid ($H_3C_4H_3O_5$) occurs (together with potassium malate) in most *unripe* fruits, especially unripe apples.

Tannic acid ($H_3C_{27}H_{19}O_{17}$—tribasic ?), or **tannin**, is found in the leaf and bark of most trees and of many shrubs (oak especially, in nut galls, hemlock, etc.), together with a little gallic acid ($H_3C_7H_3O_5$, H_2O).

THEORY OF TYPES. 125

EXP. 135.—To a solution of tannic acid add a solution of gelatin (from EXP. 134); a yellowish-white precipitate of gelatin tannate falls.

In the process of **tanning,** the tannic acid unites with the gelatin of the hide, forming a tough compound (leather).

EXP. 136.—To a solution of tannic acid add copperas solution. Ink is formed, becoming darker by exposure to the air. (*Ous* salts of Fe have a tendency to oxidize and form peculiar and, as a rule, less soluble "oxy-salts").

$$3\ \underset{\text{copperas}}{Fe\ S\ O_4}\ +\ 2\ \underset{\text{tannic acid}}{H_3C_{27}H_{19}O_{17}}\ =\ \underset{\text{INK}}{Fe_3 2\ C_{27}H_{19}O_{17}}\ +\ 3\ \underset{\text{corrodes pens}}{H_2S\ O_4}$$

Leather is blackened by washing one side with solution of iron sulphate, thus covering it with ink. Carbolic acid or corrosive sublimate ($Hg\ Cl_2$), *antiseptics*, are used to keep ink from moulding.

The **alkaloids** are organic *bases* (see comments, EXPS. 4 and 5), and they form salts on the *ammonia type*. Many of them have a bitter taste, are *powerful poisons*, and valuable medicines. (See ANTIDOTES.) The liquid alkaloids (few) contain C, H, and N, while the solid (nearly all) contain C, H, N, and O. Their salts occur in the plants from which they are obtained.

THEORY OF TYPES.

The theory of **types** has done much to advance the science of chemistry. The pupil, however, must distinguish between *theory* and *fact*. The formation of compounds on the water-type is strictly represented thus:—

$$\left.\begin{array}{c}H\\H\end{array}\right|\ O\ =\ \text{water} \qquad \left.\begin{array}{c}NO_2\\H\end{array}\right|\ O\ =\ \text{nitric acid}$$

in which the negative radical, nitryl ($N\ O_2$), replaces an atom of H in the molecule of water. So:—

$$\left.\begin{array}{c}H_2\\H_2\end{array}\right|\ O_2\ =\ \text{two molecules of water,} \qquad \left.\begin{array}{c}S\ O_2\\H_2\end{array}\right|\ O_2\ =\ \text{sulphuric acid}$$

in which two atoms of H in the water have been replaced by the negative radical sulphuryl, SO_2. The reaction in Exp. 16, written strictly to represent the water-type, becomes:—

$$\left.\begin{matrix}Na\\H\end{matrix}\right|O \;+\; \left.\begin{matrix}C_2H_3O\\H\end{matrix}\right|O \;=\; \left.\begin{matrix}C_2H_3O\\Na\end{matrix}\right|O \;+\; \left.\begin{matrix}H\\H\end{matrix}\right|O$$

It is easily seen how the negative radical, usually considered by chemists as the *replaceable* and *replacing* quantity in reactions, is obtained from the negative "grouping," viz.: by subtracting one atom of O from monad groupings, two from dyad groupings, etc. Negative radicals usually take the termination, *yl*.

Again, binary acids and salts cannot *in any strict sense* be referred to the water-type as in this book, but must be referred to the hydrochloric acid type.

The formation of compounds on the **ammonia type** is shown in the following formulas, the *connecting element* being the triad, **nitrogen**. The examples given are artificial compounds (alkaloids):—

$$\left.\begin{matrix}H\\H\\H\end{matrix}\right|N \;=\; \text{ammonia} \quad \left.\begin{matrix}C_6H_5\\H\\H\end{matrix}\right|N \;\; \begin{matrix}\text{phenyl-}\\\text{amine}\\\text{(aniline)}\end{matrix} \quad \left.\begin{matrix}C_2H_5\\H\\H\end{matrix}\right|N \;\text{ethyl-amine}$$

$$\left.\begin{matrix}C_2H_5\\C_2H_5\\H\end{matrix}\right|N \;\text{diethyl-amine} \quad \left.\begin{matrix}C_2H_5\\C_2H_5\\C_2H_5\end{matrix}\right|N \;\text{triethyl-amine}$$

If the H of ammonia (one or more atoms) is replaced by a positive radical, an *amine* results; if by a negative radical, an *amide;* if a positive and a negative both take part in the replacement, an *alkalamide*—all giving rise to very hard names.

The **ammonia type** should be considered only in this respect by beginners. Ammonia forms salts with the acids, *without replacing the hydrogen* of the acid. The alkaloids do the same thing.

EXAMPLES.

$H_3N + HCl = H_4NCl$ or H_3NHCl = chloride of ammonia
$C_6H_7N + HCl = C_6H_7NHCl$ = chloride of aniline

$C_{17}H_{19}NO_3 + HCl = C_{17}H_{19}NO_3 HCl, 3H_2O$ (water of crystallization) $= \begin{cases}\text{chloride or}\\\text{hydrochlorate}\\\text{of morphine}\end{cases}$

ALKALOIDS. 127

Morphia ($C_{17}H_{19}N\ O_3$, H_2O), or **morphine,** is the principal alkaloid in opium, the dried juice of the poppy. In small doses it acts as a *sedative;* in large doses, as a *narcotic poison.* It is combined with meconic acid in the plant as meconate of morphia. A *salt* of morphia (sulphate or chloride, usually) is sold at the drug stores as "morphia," and the same is true of many other alkaloids. **Laudanum** is tincture of opium; **paregoric,** a camphorated tincture, flavored with aromatics. Many patent concoctions for "soothing" children contain opium, and are very pernicious.

Quinia, or quinine ($C_{26}H_{24}N_2O_2$, 3 H_2O), is obtained from the bark of the cinchona, a tree found native in Peru. It is largely used in medicine, especially in **fevers.** It has a bitter taste. In large or long continued doses it is apt to *impair the hearing.*

Aconitia, or **aconite** ($C_{54}H_{46}N\ O_2$), is obtained from aconite leaves and root. It is used in **fevers** to cause perspiration (sudorific). It is one of the most violent poisons known.

Strychnia, or strychnine ($C_{21}H_{22}N_2O_2$), is the alkaloid in nux vomica (seeds) and the St. Ignatius bean. It is also one of the most poisonous of the alkaloids. It is largely used in medicine as a nervous **tonic.** It is intensely *bitter.*

Atropia ($C_{17}H_{23}N\ O_3$) exists in belladonna, or Deadly Nightshade, as malate of atropia.

Nicotia, or nicotine ($C_{10}H_{14}N_2$), is the volatile *liquid* alkaloid of the tobacco plant. It is intensely poisonous, but unfortunately, being so volatile, its smoke does not kill. The human system at length becomes tolerant of the presence of the poison, even in the stomach.

As a rule, it stupefies and clouds the intellect, especially of persons not full grown. Those boys who are great smokers rarely take a high standing in their classes.

The alkaloids are very numerous, as are also the vegetable acids. For fuller account of each see cyclopædia, also see ANTIDOTES. [Medical students should master the **tests** in APPENDIX.]

CHAPTER XXXIV.

OILS, FATS, RESINS, ETC.

There are two great classes of oils: **Fixed and Volatile** (or **Essential**). Fixed oils cannot be distilled without decomposition into various hydrocarbons. Volatile oils can be readily distilled.

Fixed oils are salts (using the term in a wide sense). Hard fat is principally glyceryl stearate ("stearin"), soft fat, glyceryl palmitate ("palmitin"), and liquid fat, glyceryl oleate ("olein"). Fixed oils, when boiled with an alkali (K, Na, etc., hydrate), react with the alkali to form a **"soap,"** and **"glycerine."** (TABLE No. 2.)

EXP. 137.—Mix a strong solution of "caustic soda" (Na H O) with olive oil and boil for about twenty minutes.

$$3\,Na\,H\,O\ +\ C_3H_5\,3\,C_{18}H_{33}O_2\ =\ 3\,Na\,C_{18}H_{33}O_2\ +\ C_3H_5\,3\,H\,O$$

sodium hydrate / glyceryl oleate (olive oil) / sodium oleate (*hard* soap, because it is not a *deliquescent* salt) / glyceryl hydrate (glycerine)

Add a little of solution of common salt. (Soap does not dissolve in salt-water.) Set aside to cool, the soap and glycerine separate.

Olive oil contains some glyceryl palmitate, so that the soap is partly sodium palmitate. If tallow be taken in place of olive oil, the soap is principally sodium stearate.

OILS, FATS, RESINS, ETC.

Inspection of the reaction reveals the whole story of soap-making. If "caustic potash" is taken, the reaction becomes

$$3 \text{ K H O} + \underset{\text{glyceryl oleate}}{C_3H_5\, 3\, C_{18}H_{33}O_2} = \underset{\substack{\text{soft soap, because} \\ \text{potassium oleate is} \\ \text{a deliquescent salt}}}{3 \text{ K } C_{18}H_{33}O_2} + \underset{\text{glycerine}}{C_3H_5\, 3\, H\, O}$$
_{caustic potash}

Potassium forms a soft soap and sodium a hard soap. Ca forms an insoluble "lime soap." Mg also forms an insoluble soap. Insoluble soaps are sometimes used in medicine and in the arts. Solutions of soluble soaps (K and Na) are good *solvents* of the cuticle and of many forms of "dirt," and hence are valuable cleansing agents. They must be used, however, with soft water, or there is a great waste of the soap. If soft soap, for instance, is put into hard water (*e. g.*, containing Ca S O$_4$, or other soluble sulphate), the soap is destroyed, and an insoluble "lime soap" formed by the following reaction:—

$$\text{Ca S O}_4 + \underset{\text{soft soap}}{2 \text{ K } C_{18}H_{33}O_2} = K_2S O_4 + \underset{\text{insoluble lime soap}}{\text{Ca } 2\, C_{18}H_{33}O_2}$$

A similar reaction takes place if the water is only of temporary hardness. (See EXP. 33.) Water of temporary hardness, as we have seen, is softened *by boiling*. Water of permanent hardness may be softened (for washing purposes) by adding borax (Na$_2$B$_4$O$_7$), or washing soda (Na$_2$C O$_3$, 10 H$_2$O). If the last,

$$\underset{\substack{\text{cause of} \\ \text{hardness}}}{\text{Ca S O}_4} + Na_2C O_3 = \underset{\substack{\text{(remaining in solu lon} \\ \text{but not affecting} \\ \text{the soap)}}}{Na_2 S O_4} + \underset{\text{precipitate}}{\text{Ca C O}_3}$$

In making **"lye"** from wood ashes, the ashes are leached in a large tub containing "lime" (Ca 2 H O) at the bottom. The K$_2$C O$_3$ of the ashes is carried by the hot water down through lime, and the reaction is:—

$$\text{Ca 2 H O} + K_2C O_3 = \underset{\text{"lye"}}{2 K H O} + \text{Ca C O}_3$$

130 CHEMICAL PRIMER.

If no lime is used, of course the lye is potassium carbonate (impure solution), and in making soap from K_2CO_3 we have (if olive oil is used) [Don't try to remember reaction.]

$$3 K_2CO_3 + 3 H_2O + 2 C_3H_5 3 C_{18}H_{33}O_2 = 6 K C_{18}H_{33}O_2 \text{ (soap)} + 2 C_3H_5 3 H O \text{ (glycerine)} + 3 CO_2$$

Soap usually contains an excess of the alkali. Home-made soap contains both alkali and glycerine and is very variable in its composition, containing several fat acids united to the alkali. Soap is insoluble in salt-water and hence separates if salt be added to the "suds."

"Stearin" candles are made (chiefly) of stearic acid by decomposing the tallow by superheated (285°) steam.

$$3 H_2O \text{ (steam)} + C_3H_5 3 C_{18}H_{35}O_2 \text{ (tallow)} = 3 H C_{18}H_{35}O_2 \text{ (stearic acid (stearin candles))} + C_3H_5 3 H O \text{ (glycerine)}$$

There are two great classes of fixed oils, **drying** oils and **non-drying** oils. A drying oil (as linseed oil, *i. e.*, flax-seed oil), when exposed to the air, oxidizes to a hard resinous substance. A non-drying oil does not oxidize to a resinous body when exposed to the air, but instead suffers a fermentation that sets the acid of the oil free, that is, the oil becomes "*rancid*." For instance, the purest olive oil is not entirely free from nitrogenous material, and fungus germs, creeping in, cause the following reaction:—

$$C_3H_5 3 C_{18}H_{33}O_2 \text{ (olive oil)} + 3 H_2O \text{ (moisture from air)} = 3 H C_{18}H_{33}O_2 \text{ (oleic acid)} + C_3H_5 3 H O \text{ (glycerine)}$$

As we have seen, **glycerine** ($C_3H_5 3 H O$) is a "*by-product*" in the manufacture of soap. **Glycerine** is classed by chemists as an alcohol. It is a viscid, sweet liquid, a good solvent, and a valuable *antiseptic*. It is useful in dressing wounds, because it is not volatile, but protects from the air and keeps the part moist. Glycerine, treated with nitric and sulphuric acids, becomes the fearful explosive *nitro-glycerine* ($C_3H_5 3 N O_3$, glyceryl nitrate).

CHEMISTRY OF CLEANING.

The **soaps** stand first in the list of cleansing agents, their solution in soft water (preferably hot) dissolving or forming emulsions with oily substances. The sebaceous glands of the skin secrete oleaginous matter to keep the skin soft and pliable (there is also oily matter in the perspiration). This oil, with accompanying "dirt," being absorbed by the clothing prevents water alone from cleansing the material, as "oil and water will not mix."

Solutions of **caustic potash** and **caustic soda** form emulsions with oils even more readily than soaps do, but they corrode the skin and are apt to injure the cloth as well. Dilute solutions are used to clean window glass, greasy tins, etc.

Wood ashes (which contain potassium carbonate) are used with water to cleanse bottles and coarse utensils. Solutions of potassium carbonate operate like solutions of caustic potash only with much less intensity.

Ammonia water is the best agent for cleaning glass and (purified) for cleansing woolens and for the bath, also very dilute for hair brushes.

Sal soda (washing soda, sodium carbonate) is used to soften hard water (see above) and also is useful with soft water. In the latter case not over two ounces (*first dissolved*) should be added to a large tub of water. It injures the skin if too strong and does not cleanse so effectively. So-called "washing compounds" are composed principally of sodium carbonate.

Solutions of **borax** are excellent to cleanse delicate and *colored* fabrics. They also soften water permanently hard (see above).

To dissolve oily spots, **benzine** (a volatile oil from petroleum), fresh, pure turpentine, alcohol, and ether are used. Solid *absorbents* are often to be preferred to remove spots from paper, carpets, etc., such as **magnesium carbonate,** powdered soapstone, and buckwheat flour. These should be several times thoroughly rubbed into the carpet or upon the paper and then brushed out or off again.

Grass stains are removed (*while fresh*) by dissolving in **absolute alcohol.** Fruit stains are washed away by pouring on *boiling* water, or, if this fails, by solution of oxalic acid.

Iron rust (red) is best removed by several applications of hot, very dilute **hydrochloric acid,** soluble chloride of iron being formed by "change of partners." Thoroughly wash afterward with water. "Soluble blues" are composed principally of iron ferrocyanide (Prussian blue), and clothes should be thoroughly rinsed to remove the alkali, or iron rust stains appear by decomposition of the "bluing."

Ink (black iron stains) is removed by solution of **oxalic acid**, chemical reaction by "change of partners" gives iron oxalate and tannic acid. Immediately and thoroughly wash out with water and finally with very dilute ammonia water, else a yellowish tannic acid stain is left.

Oxalic acid is also an excellent agent for cleansing brass, removing "shoe-leather" stains, etc.

Fumes of **burning sulphur** (SO_2, which see) will often remove colored spots when nothing else will.

Acetic acid added to the second rinsing water will restore perfectly the color (if from "coal-tar" dye) of bright blue flannels or other fabrics that fade somewhat in washing, because the soap neutralizes partially the acid contained in the dye. [See "AMMONIA WATER," page 62.]

Coarse scouring agents are easily obtained, but for silver and articles of value, the best polishing agent is, perhaps, precipitated chalk. Five cents' worth of quicklime and ten cents' worth of hydrochloric acid by the process of EXP. 33, will precipitate sufficient to last for a long time. The water used should be filtered, and after quicklime is slacked, the clear lime water should be carefully drawn off by siphon so as to exclude all *gritty* sediment. After precipitation carefully dry and preserve. Many polishing agents, for a tablespoonful of which twenty-five cents is asked, are principally, if not entirely, precipitated chalk. Most "tooth powders" are simply precipitated chalk (colored and perfumed).

Volatile oils (or **Essential oils**) are of vegetable origin. They exist in the petals of flowers, in leaves (of mint), in seeds (of carraway), in rind of fruit (of orange, lemon) and in the root (of sassafras). They are usually obtained by distilling with water (passing steam over), from the part of the plant containing them. They do not make soaps. Their "solution" in alcohol is called an **essence**. Adulteration with a fixed oil is easily discovered by evaporating on white paper and noticing that a *grease spot* is left.

Oil of Turpentine ($C_{10}H_{16}$ "spirits of turpentine") is obtained from the "pitch" of pines by distillation. It is an excellent *solvent*, dissolving the resins to form *varnishes*. A large class of volatile oils are pure hydro-carbons, many having the same empirical formula with oil of turpentine, though widely different in properties.

Of a second class Camphor ($C_{10}H_{16}O$) is a type, as oil of bitter almonds, cinnamon, spearmint, etc. These all contain O.

A third class of *"strong smelling"* volatile oils contain S. Ex: Oil of mustard, horse-radish, onion, etc.

A **resin** is an essential oil oxidized. (**"Rosin"** is the resin of turpentine.) A **balsam** is an oleo-resin, *i. e.*, a resin dissolved in a volatile oil, or a volatile oil partially oxidized. If a balsam is distilled, the essential oil passes over, leaving the resin behind. **Shellac** is a resin obtained from lac, the juice of an East India tree. (See APPENDIX.) **Amber** is a fossil resin.

Gum resins are milky exudations from many plants, which afterward solidify in the air. **Gutta-percha** is obtained from the juice of an East India tree, as is also **gum-benzoin,** the chief source of benzoic acid ($H C_7H_5O_2$). **India-rubber** (caoutchouc) is the solidified juice of certain tropical trees. Vulcanized rubber is made by heating the rubber with sulphur (Goodyear's patent).

CHAPTER XXXV.

ANTIDOTES.

When a person is taken suddenly and violently ill after eating something, poisoning may be suspected. By careful attention to this chapter it is more than possible that some member of the class may be able to save a human life.

A **poison** is a substance which, if introduced into the animal system, may produce morbid or deadly effects. We give antidotes, either (1) *to get rid of the poison at once* (by means of an emetic, or cathartic—a mechanical antidote), or (2) *to hinder its absorption* (as when we give a chemical antidote to form an insoluble compound with the poison—see EXP. 12), or (3) *to counteract its effect* (as when we give stimulants for the poison of serpent bites, for narcotic poisons, etc.).

EXP. 138.—Shake up thoroughly the white of an egg in a bottle half filled with water and filter. The filtrate is a solution of albumen. Arrange test tubes containing *very slightly acid* solution of soluble compounds of Hg (corrosive sublimate), Cu. Zn, Sn, Fe (copperas), Ag (nitrate), [Pb and Ba] respectively. Into each let fall two or three drops of albumen solution. Insoluble compounds of albumen and the metal (formula too complex to be written) are precipitated. [Notice that with Pb and Ba compounds the precipitate does not readily appear and antidotes *below* are to be relied upon.]

Albumen (milk, flour and water, and especially **raw eggs)** is an excellent chemical antidote for most metallic salts. As precipitates are not absolutely insoluble *in the stomach*, they should be immediately removed by an **emetic.**

The best emetic is the common one, "mustard" (a teaspoonful in a cup of—preferably warm—water). Whenever poisons are to be removed by an emetic, warm water should be freely drank to rinse out the stomach thoroughly. **Oils** (fats, butter, and lard) and mucilaginous drinks (as flaxseed tea) **are always beneficial** and should be freely given immediately, and for treatment afterward. In general, whatever would be good treatment for a *burned, bruised, or injured skin*, is good treatment *for the mucous membrane of the alimentary canal*, burned or irritated by some poison.

If silver nitrate or corrosive sublimate are *strong*, the antidote must be given *within a few seconds*, or the poison will have done its worst, and recovery, if it takes place at all, must depend upon after treatment. A

ANTIDOTES.

rather large dose of a mild cathartic (as castor oil) should be used instead of the emetic whenever solution of either sublimate or nitrate has been taken. The best antidote for silver nitrate is salt and water, as we have inferred from EXP. 6, though albumen is about as good.

If the other metallic salts (except, see cyanides below) have been swallowed, especially in the solid state (powder), the antidote may be given later (from ten to twenty minutes) with hope of its doing good. But *the danger rapidly increases with the lapse of time.*

Most salts of Zn and Sb (also $CuSO_4$) are fortunately emetics themselves, but if vomiting does not occur, prompt action must be resorted to. The best antidote for zinc, copper, or iron sulphate is a careful dose of sodium carbonate, "washing soda" (followed by emetic).

$$ZnSO_4 + Na_2CO_3 = Na_2SO_4 + \underset{\text{insoluble}}{ZnCO_3}$$

The best antidote for "arsenic" (or Sb) is fresh, moist ferric hydrate, $Fe_2 6HO$. It is best precipitated when needed by mixing ferric chloride solution (liquor or tincture) with slight excess of dilute ammonia water. An insoluble ferric arsenate ($Fe_2 2AsO_4$) is formed in the stomach. Chalk, oil, milk, or mucilaginous drinks may be given to envelop the particles of As_2O_3 mechanically, if it has been taken in the solid form; *but the thing to be depended upon ordinarily is the* **emetic,** followed by purgative (castor oil).

A careful dose of potassium ferrocyanide is a good antidote for copper compounds, as $Cu_2Fe(CN)_6$ is insoluble (give emetic).

Magnesium sulphate (Epsom salt, EXP. 12) is the best antidote for lead and barium compounds (*with emetic*).

A careful dose of ammonium carbonate is the best antidote for tin compounds (with emetic).

Example:—

$$SnCl_2 + (H_4N)_2CO_3 + H_2O = 2H_4NCl + \underset{\text{precipitate}}{Sn 2HO} + CO_2$$

The antidote for **acids** (sulphuric, nitric, hydrochloric, etc.) is **magnesium carbonate** (see REACTION, CLASS 4), chalk, **lime-water,** or soapsuds. The antidote must be given within *a few seconds* if the acids are strong.

For oxalic acid, lime-water (Exp. 15, or chalk) is the best antidote. Prussic acid (K C N) and other cyanides require stimulants, as cold douche to the spine, *dilute* ammonia water inhaled and ammonium carbonate given in *small doses* (see snake poison below). If prussic acid is strong there is no antidote. **Give no emetics with acids** (unless acid is *very dilute*), but administer oil (olive) freely.

The antidote for **alkalies** (caustic potash, "lye," caustic soda, etc.) is a dilute acid, preferably the most common one **vinegar** (acetic).

$$K H O \ + \ H C_2 H_3 O_2 \ = \ \underset{\substack{\text{soluble but} \\ \text{harmless salt}}}{K C_2 H_3 O_2} \ + \ H_2 O$$

Or tartaric acid, "cream of tartar," citric acid (lemon juice), etc. If these are not at hand and the mineral acids are given, the acid must be very dilute and given sparingly. *An overdose would be substituting one poison for another.* (For caustic baryta, Ba 2 H O, or for lead hydrate, see above.)

If the caustic alkalies are strong, the antidote must follow *in a few seconds*, or it will be of no avail. **Give no emetic with alkalies.**

For **narcotic poisons** (as opium, morphine, cholera medicines, "soothing syrups") and the **alkaloids** in general, the **emetic is to be relied upon** chiefly, though *tannic acid* (strong tea or **coffee**) may be given, as it forms an insoluble compound with many alkaloids.

The narcotic poisons require in addition to the emetic, *stimulants* (strong **coffee,** brandy, careful dose of ammonium carbonate) and vigorous efforts to *keep the patient awake.* Strong *coffee* is especially useful in cases of opium poisoning, as it acts as a powerful stimulant to the nerve centers affected by opium. *Aconite* calls for *stimulants. Strychnine* requires above all the *emetic,* also the inhalation of chloroform or ether to check spasms. Patient must be kept as *quiet as possible.*

The **emetic** should be promptly given in case of poisoning by **unhealthy fish or meat.** Oils should follow (and paregoric in severe cases).

ANTIDOTES.

Phosphorus poisoning requires the **emetic** and mucilaginous drinks with magnesium hydrate (best precipitated when needed by adding ammonium hydrate to slight *excess* of magnesium sulphate solution), followed by large doses of the **cathartic** (purgative) castor oil.

It is not generally known that **"carbolic acid"** (remember that this is not an *acid* proper, but an alcohol) is a more dangerous poison than strychnine. Strychnine kills "deliberately" and with a smaller dose, but carbolic acid does its work *quick*. Strychnine gives time (10 to even 30 minutes) to hunt up antidotes, or call a physician; but if a teaspoonful of strong carbolic acid is taken, usually no remedy will save a life after *twenty seconds* have elapsed. As it is frequently used in sick rooms for bathing purposes (diluted), its well known odor is no protection in such cases. **Olive oil** (butter, lard, etc.) freely given, followed by **castor oil** (cathartic) is its best antidote. **Give no emetic.**

For the bite of **poisonous serpents** (poison, a powerful sedative), stimulants, as alcoholic liquors, but best of all, ammonium carbonate (a teaspoonful of 10 per cent. solution, which may be carried in a small vial, *tightly corked*, in the vest pocket) should be taken *within a few seconds*. The dose of ammonium carbonate should be repeated twice at intervals of ten minutes. If possible, the wound should be immediately canterized (by nitric acid, caustic potash, or hot wire), or ligature put about the limb above, and the poison sucked out from the wound (the poison is harmless in the stomach).

NOTE.—The pupil will notice that in most cases of poisoning the **emetic** is given. He should charge his memory with the few exceptions, *acids*, *alkalies* (also silver nitrate, corrosive sublimate), and *carbolic acid*, and give emetics in all other cases. To receive poisons into an empty stomach is most dangerous. In a full stomach the poison is diluted and the absorption is slow, so that rapid filling of the stomach with almost any liquid food would be better than nothing. Especially would milk and mucilaginous drinks be useful dilutents, to say nothing of their soothing action. A physician should be called in all cases of serious poisoning to direct the after-treatment.

The following statements about poisons should be carefully studied and observed at your homes:—

1. Poisons should never be left within the reach of children.

2. They should be kept by themselves, apart from non-poisonous medicines.

3. They should be kept *plainly labeled* as **poison**.

4. Any substance in an unlabeled bottle should be promptly destroyed.

5. *Whenever a poison is bought, its antidote should be bought,* placed beside it and plainly labeled (as to the proper dose, if antidote in excess would be injurious).

6. After this last is done it should be remembered that "an ounce of prevention is worth a hundred pounds of cure."

MISCELLANEOUS QUESTIONS.

1. Matter exists in what three physical states?
2. The atomic theory divides matter how?
3. Atoms of different elements differ in what three essential respects?
4. Define compound radical, acid, base, salt, precipitate, reagent, filtrate, sand bath, water bath, alkali, sublimation.
5. What is "soda water"? Davy's safety lamp? a deliquescent substance? a condenser? a pipette? oil of vitriol? aqua regia?
6. How much mercury in 150 grams of mercuric sulphide (use tables)?
7. How much lead will be required to make 250 kgs. of lead carbonate? How much to make 25 grams of PbO?
8. How much silver nitrate was in a solution from which 30 gms. of silver chloride was precipitated?
9. Write formulas for ferric oxide, cuprous oxide, mercuric nitrate, ferrous sulphide, cupric chloride, aluminum oxide, mercurous iodide, stannic chloride, ferrous sulphate, and ferric sulphate?
10. Reaction when calcium carbonate and citric acid are united.
11. Reaction in making oxygen, hydrogen, carbon dioxide, hydrogen sulphide, hydrochloric acid, and sulphur dioxide.

MISCELLANEOUS QUESTIONS. 139

12. How many litres of O can be made from 300 gms. of potassium chlorate? (A litre of H weighs .0896 gms.)
13. If we obtain 500 litres of CO_2, how much calcium carbonate was used? How might the druggist make $Cu\ C_4 H_4 O_6$?
14. Tell what you know of SO_2 (3 lines), of oxygen, of nitrogen.
15. Tell what you know of H_2S, of H, of CO_2, of Cl, of CN.
16. What is glass? How annealed? How colored? How etched?
17. How might you tell whether or not a white powder was As_2O_3?
18. Give Marsh's test for "arsenic." How told from antimony?
19. What is an alloy? an amalgam? metal? "paste" diamonds?
20. What three methods of "mining for gold?" and tell much more about each than you find in this Primer (10 lines).
21. For what is platinum used? phosphorus? borax? mercury?
22. What would you do if you had taken by mistake nitrate of Ag?
23. How would you test for decomposing organic matter?
24. Why can some metals be cast, while others cannot?
25. What is "white lead," and how made? What is mosaic gold?
26. What is the antidote for lead acetate? barium hydrate? carbolic acid? corrosive sublimate? oxalic acid? phosphorous?
27. Give Bessemer's process for making steel. Leblanc's process for Na_2CO_3. How would the druggist make calcium citrate?
28. What is "galvanized iron?" "tinware?" quicklime? plaster of Paris? quartz? a "base metal"? an oxidizing agent?
29. What is fusible metal? indelible ink? gelatin? leather?
30. Difference between water-slacked and air-slacked lime?
31. Give reaction in making soft soap (use TABLE); hard soap.
32. How is brown sugar refined? Name *five* prominent alkaloids.
33. Reactions in alcoholic and acetic fermentations ($C_6H_{12}O_6$ sugar).
34. Why is soap wasted when hard water is used in washing?
35. What is a resin? rosin? a balsam? tincture? essence? soap?
36. What would you do if one had taken an overdose of morphine?
37. In what cases of poisoning should no emetic be given?
38. What makes the bread "rise?" Explain fully.
39. Name all the antiseptics mentioned in this book.
40. Name the disinfectants; the anæsthetics; the bleaching agents.

APPENDIX.

SECTION A.

NORMAL SALTS, ACID SALTS, ETC.

A **normal salt** (old name neutral salt) is one which is formed by replacing all the replaceable hydrogen of the acid by a positive element or grouping.

EXAMPLE.

$H_2C_4H_4O_6$ = hydrogen tartrate = acid.
$K_2C_4H_4O_6$ = potassium tartrate = normal salt.

NOTE.—Hitherto by salts have been meant normal salts.

An **acid salt** is one which is formed by replacing only part of the replaceable hydrogen of the acid by a positive element or grouping.

EXAMPLE.

$H_2C_4H_4O_6$ = hydrogen tartrate = acid.

$HKC_4H_4O_6$ = $\begin{cases} \text{hydrogen potassium tartrate} \\ \text{or acid potassium tartrate} \end{cases}$ = acid salt.

Acid salts usually turn blue litmus red, but this is by no means universal. In Exp. 39, if one-half as much sodium nitrate be taken, with strong sulphuric acid, an acid salt, instead of a normal salt, results.

$$NaNO_3 + H_2SO_4 = \underset{\substack{\text{acid} \\ \text{sodium} \\ \text{sulphate}}}{HNaSO_4} + HNO_3$$

APPENDIX. 141

In general, by adding an excess of the acid (which is the same as taking less of the other substance), an acid salt may be obtained. Acid salts, as a rule, react with carbonates like acids, that is, forming a *salt* (normal), *water*, and *carbon dioxide*, as:—

$$2\ H\ K\ C_4H_4O_6 \underset{\text{acid salt}}{} +\ K_2CO_3 \underset{\text{carbonate}}{} =\ 2\ K_2C_4H_4O_6 \underset{\text{normal salt}}{} +\ H_2O \underset{\text{water}}{} +\ CO_2 \underset{\text{carbon dioxide}}{}$$

A double salt is one which is formed by replacing part or all of the replaceable hydrogen of the acid by two positive elements or groupings.

EXAMPLE.

$H_2C_4H_4O_6$ = tartaric acid.

K Na $C_4H_4O_6$ = potassium sodium tartrate = double salt. ("Rochelle salt")

H_3PO_4 = phosphoric acid.

H Na H_4 N P O_4 = hydrogen sodium ammonium phosphate = double salt (microcosmic salt). A double salt may be at the same time an acid salt, like the last.

A double salt may be formed by an acid salt of one metal acting on the carbonate of the other, thus:—

$$Na_2CO_3 \underset{\text{sodium carbonate}}{} +\ 2\ H\ K\ C_4H_4O_6 \underset{\substack{\text{acid}\\\text{potassium}\\\text{tartrate}}}{} =\ 2\ K\ Na\ C_4H_4O_6 \underset{\text{double salt}}{} +\ H_2O \underset{\text{water}}{} +\ CO_2 \underset{\text{carbon dioxide}}{}$$

Acids containing one, two, three, etc., atoms of replaceable hydrogen are said to be respectively **monobasic, dibasic, tribasic,** etc.

HNO_3 = monobasic acid.

H_2SO_4 = dibasic acid.

H_3PO_4 = tribasic acid.

H_4SiO_4 = tetrabasic acid.

NOTE.—A tribasic acid may form *two* acid salts, as:—

$H_2Na\ PO_4$ = dihydrogen sodium phosphate = acid salt.

$H\ Na_2P\ O_4$ = hydrogen disodium phosphate = acid salt.

A basic salt is one which may be formed by replacing one or more hydrate groupings of the base by a negative grouping. [This definition is a narrow one, covering most but not all basic salts. It may be, however, that basic salts are molecular compounds of the hydrate (or oxide) of the metal with the metallic salt, the hydrate uniting after the analogy of water of crystallization.]

EXAMPLE.

Pb 2 H O = lead hydrate = base.
Pb H O N O_3 = lead hydro-nitrate = basic salt.
Al_2 6 H O = aluminum hydrate = base.
Al_2 (H O)$_2$ Si O_4 = aluminum hydro-silicate = basic salt.
Bi 3 H O = bismuth hydrate = base.
Bi (H O)$_2$ N O_3 = { basic bismuth nitrate, "subnitrate of bismuth," used largely in medicine.

Sulph- and selen-acids and salts. In all formulas for ternaries thus far explained, oxygen has been the last element. It is supposed to be principally a *linking* or *connecting* element. Now there are a few other dyad elements that can perform this office of linking, especially **sulphur and selenium.** To write the formula for a sulph- or a selen-acid or salt, the same reference table may be used, only sulphur or selenium, as the case may be, must be substituted *atom for atom*, in place of oxygen.

EXAMPLE.

K_2C O_3 = potassium carbonate = salt.
K_2C S_3 = potassium sulpho-carbonate = sulph-salt.
Ag_3 As O_4 = silver arsenate = salt.
Ag_3 As S_4 = silver sulph-arsenate = sulph-salt.
K_3 Sb O_3 = potassium antimonite = salt.
K_3 Sb S_3 = potassium selen-antimonite = selen-salt.
H_3 As S_4 = hydrogen sulph-arsenate = sulph-acid.

NOTE.—Instead of sulph-, thio- (Greek *thion*, sulphur) is used by some chemists, as K_2C S_3 = potassium thio-carbonate.

The sulph- and selen-acids and salts are few compared to those containing oxygen.

APPENDIX. 143

SECTION B.

THE ALLOY, SPECTRUM ANALYSIS, AND SYSTEMS OF CRYSTALLIZATION.

The most important **alloys** (with their usual proportions) are:—

Aluminum Bronze............................	Cu (9) Al (1)
Bell-metal..................................	Cu (9) Sn (2)
Brass......................................	Cu (2) Zn (1)
Bronze....................................	Cu (95) Sn (4) Zn (1)
Coin (gold)................................	Au (90) Cu (9) Ag (1)
Coin (silver)..............................	Ag (9) Cu (1)
Fusible Metal..............................	Bi (see) Pb Sn
German Silver..............................	Cu (5) Zn (2) Ni (2)
	‿brass‿
Hard Solder................................	Cu (1) Zn (1)
Pewter.....................................	Sn (4) Pb (1)
Phosphor-bronze............................	Cu (88) Sn (10) P (1.5) Pb (.5)
Shot.......................................	Pb (99.5) As (.5)
Soft Solder................................	Pb (1) Sn (1)
Type-metal.................................	Pb (70) Sb (20) Sn (10)

The **spectroscope,** next to the balance, is the most useful instrument for original chemical research. It consists of a **prism,** mounted upon a stand, carrying a tube with fine, adjustable slit, through which light (the rays being made parallel by a lens) falls upon the prism. The light, refracted by the prism, is received by a small telescope, which magnifies the **spectrum** ("rainbow," if solar spectrum, *i. e.*, if light is sunlight) before it reaches the eye. The spectrum of the sun has dark lines (**Fraunhofer's lines**), crossing it at right angles all along from the red to the violet portion, but at irregular intervals. The relative position of these lines has been accurately determined.

144 CHEMICAL PRIMER.

If, instead of sunlight, the light from the sodium flame (EXP. 130) enters the slit, no colored bands from red to violet, as in the solar spectrum, are seen. Instead, the spectrum is totally dark except a brilliant *yellow* line (double) crossing the spectrum where before (in solar spectrum) was the dark line D (double). If the light of the potassium flame enter the slit, three lines appear on the dark spectrum: a bright purplish line at (what was before) the violet end, and at the other end two red lines—one somewhat bright, the other very faint.

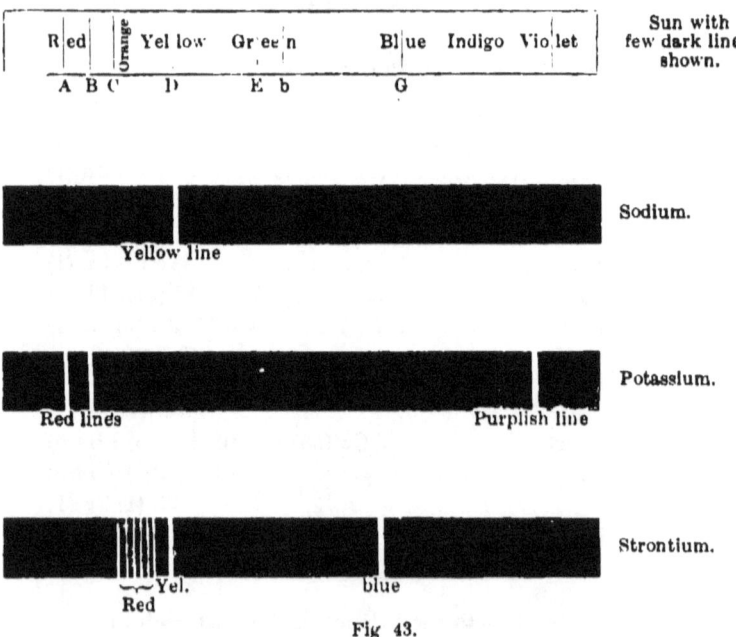

Fig. 43.

All the other metals and non-metals have characteristic spectra, but some substances require more heat than the flame of the Bunsen's burner to volatilize them. For these the electric flame is used. With a small spectroscope, however, the student can easily obtain the spectra of Na, K, Ba, Sr, and Ca, whose chlorides are volatilized in Bunsen's or alcohol flame. [See Fig. 43. For some laboratory spectroscopes, spectra are reversed and Fig. 43 must be turned upside down to represent the view.]

APPENDIX. 145

Many rare metals have been discovered by means of the spectroscope (cæsium, rubidium, thallium, indium, etc.). By it the light of the heavenly bodies reveals the presence in these orbs of many elements common upon the earth. (Celestial Chemistry.)

Most chemical substances, when they pass from the liquid to the solid state, assume some definite form and are said to **crystallize**. (See EXP. 34 and connection.) It has been found possible to arrange all crystals in **six systems**, according to the arrangement of their sides and angles around certain imaginary **axes**, intersecting at the center of the crystals. These axes are shown only in Plates I and II of Fig. 44.

1. **Regular System.**—Three axes all *equal* and all at *right* angles. Plates I, II, and III. Ex.: Common salt, alum, garnet.

2. **Hexagonal System.**—Four axes, three equal and in one plane, making angles of 60°, and one, longer or shorter, at right angles to the plane of the other three. Plates IV and V. Ex.: Sodium nitrate, quartz, and ice.

3. **Quadratic System.**—Three axes all at right angles, and one shorter or longer than the other two. Plates VI and VII. Ex.: Potassium ferrocyanide and tin dioxide.

4. **Rhombic System.**—Three axes all unequal and all at right angles. Plates VIII and IX. Ex.: Potassium nitrate, barium sulphate, and sulphur, *crystallized from solution in carbon bisulphide*.

5. **Monoclinic System.**—Three axes all unequal. Two cut each other obliquely, and one is at right angles to the plane of the other two. Plate X. Ex.: Sodium carbonate, sodium phosphate, ferrous sulphate, borax, cane-sugar, and sulphur *from fusion*.

6. **Triclinic System.**—Three axes, all unequal and all oblique. Plates XI and XII. Ex.: Copper sulphate, manganese sulphate, boracic acid and potassium bichromate.

Certain substances, like S, crystallize in two systems, and are said to be *dimorphous*. A very few substances are trimorphous. Anything without crystalline form is *amorphous* (as *plastic* sulphur). Different substances that crystallize in the same form are *isomorphous* (as compounds of the halogens with the same metal). A crystalline body splits more readily in a certain direction than others. This splitting is called *cleavage*. The powder of a crushed or scratched mineral is called its *streak*.

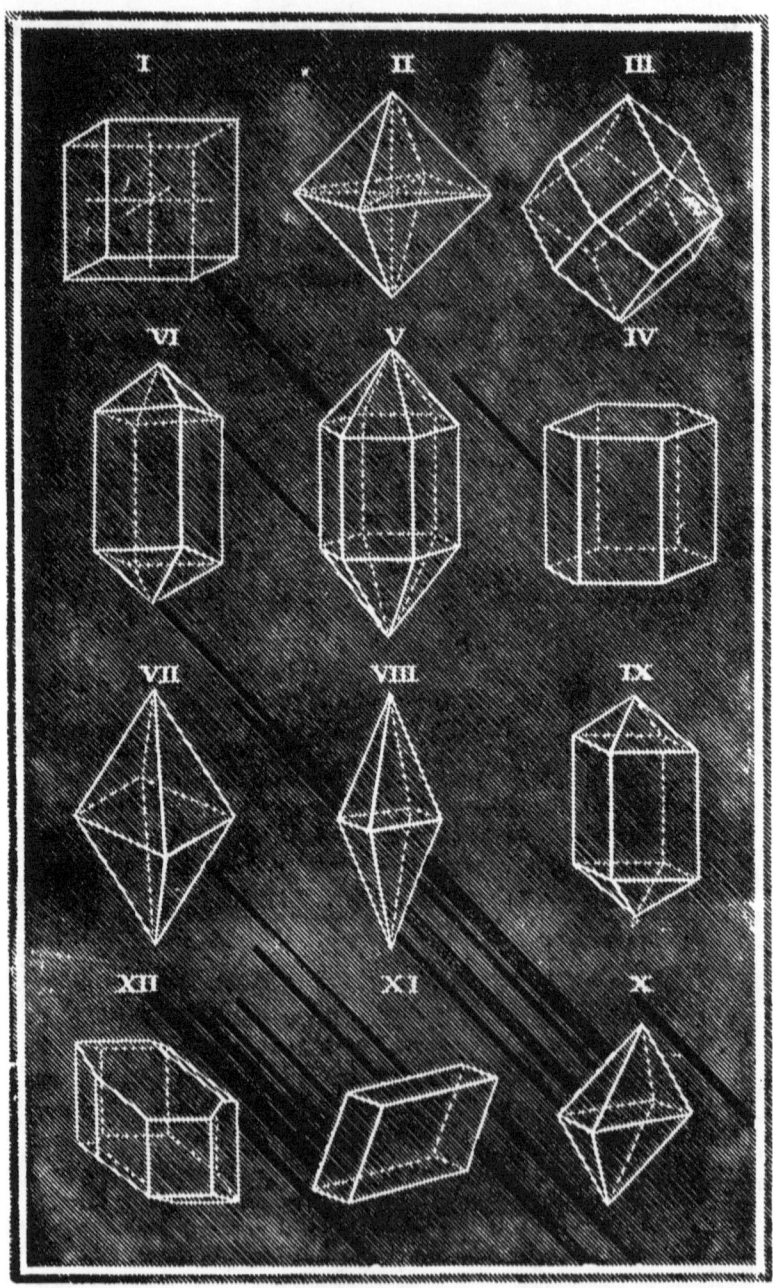

Fig. 44.

APPENDIX. 147

SECTION C.

DYEING.

Exp. 1.—Dissolve a little aniline blue ($C_{20}H_{16}(C_6H_5)_3N_3$) in alcohol, and dip clean, white silk thread into it. Expose the thread to the air, the alcohol evaporates and leaves the blue color adherent to every fiber of the silk.

Aniline ($C_6H_5H_2N$) is a volatile, oily liquid; colorless, when pure, but by oxidation, *action of chemical agents*, etc., aniline black, red (magenta), orange, yellow, green, blue, and violet (mauve) are produced. The *reactions* in the formation of the wonderful "aniline dyes" are by far too complex for introduction here.

Exp. 2.—Upon fine zinc filings in a beaker place a minute quantity of blue indigo, add a moderately strong solution of potassium hydrate (potash) and heat.

(a)—$Zn + 2 K H O = K Zn O_2 + \underset{\text{nascent}}{H_2}$

(b)—$\underset{\substack{\text{reducing} \\ \text{agent}}}{H_2} + \underset{\text{blue indigo}}{C_{16}H_{10}N_2O_2} = \underset{\text{white indigo}}{C_{16}H_{12}N_2O_2}$

Dip a piece of clean, white woolen (or cotton) cloth in the solution of white indigo and expose to the air, blue indigo is formed in its fibers by oxidation and adheres, that is, is a *"fast"* color (does not wash out in warm soap-suds).

$\underset{\text{white indigo}}{C_{16}H_{12}N_2O_2} + O = \underset{\text{blue indigo}}{C_{16}H_{10}N_2O_2} + \underset{\text{evaporates}}{H_2O}$

Exp. 3.—Divide a dilute (1 per cent.) solution of **picric acid** ($C_6H_3N_3O_{10}$) into two portions. Into one dip a piece of woolen yarn, into the other dip cotton yarn. Remove each and wash. The first is dyed a brilliant yellow, the second is not colored.

Substances that dye directly are called *substantive colors*. Coloring substances may form colored compounds with the fibers of the cloth, or (usually) may merely adhere to the fibers. Cotton and linen often require different treatment from wool or silk to produce the same color, and, in general, are dyed with more difficulty.

EXP. 4.—Divide a solution of *alum* into two parts. To the first add $H_4 N H O$, a flocculent precipitate of aluminum hydrate ($Al_2 6 H O$) falls. To the second add a few drops of solution of *cochineal (carmine ink)*, and then $H_4 N H O$. $Al_2 6 H O$ is precipitated as before, and *slowly* settles, *carrying the coloring matter down with it*, forming a "**lake.**"

Some other metallic hydrates (or oxides), especially of tin and of iron, have the same great affinity for organic coloring matter. The compounds they form with coloring matters are called *lakes*. The hydrates also have "great affinity for" (adherence to) the fibers of cloth. Every one knows that, though "dirt" can be readily washed from a white apron, iron rust is removed with great difficulty (only by chemical agents—see CHEMISTRY OF CLEANING). Hydrates (or salts, from which the hydrates may be produced) that have a great affinity for coloring matter and also for the fiber of cloth, are called *mordants*, and a color that will not dye directly, but needs a mordant, is called an *adjective color*.

Coloring by means of **mordants** is the usual method. The most common mordants are copperas, tin salts, and alum. The cloth is first dipped into a solution of the mordant and then into the dye. Of course different mordants produce different colors, when used with the same dye. The mordants may be applied by means of stamps (or rollers) and any pattern (as for calico) brought out in the various colors.

EXP. 5.—Boil a piece of $Fe S O_4$ in nitric acid (90 per cent.), till red fumes cease to appear; dilute and filter. Preserve filtrate ($Fe_2 3 S O_4$, "persulphate of iron"). Dip *clean* silk into this ferric sulphate (mordant) and leave for a few minutes. Drain, and immerse in solution of potassium ferrocyanide (dye). It is colored a deep blue (Prussian blue).

$2 Fe_2 3 S O_4$ + $3 K_4 Fe (C N)_6$ = $6 K_2 S O_4$ + $(Fe_2)_2 3 Fe (C N)_6$
  mordant   dye   ferric ferrocyanide
                                                                                     Prussian blue

The reactions of the organic dyes with their mordants are too complex to be written out. Indeed, many of them are unknown. The most common coloring substances are *madder* (coloring principle alizarin, now made artificially from coal-tar), cochineal (dried insects from cactus of Central America, coloring principle, *carmine*), logwood, indigo, litmus, etc. (See DYEING, in cyclopædia.)

APPENDIX. 149

SECTION D.

ADDITIONAL EXPERIMENTS.

HYDROGEN AND OXYGEN.

EXP. 1.—Repeat EXP. 30 with a test-tube of the right size and the H flame "sings." It sets the column of air in vibration within the test-tube.

EXP. 2.—Ignite a small jet of H by holding in it platinum sponge (previously heated to expel absorbed gases which hinder the action).

EXP. 3.—Place a sounding tuning-fork in a jar of H; the tone is raised to a shrill pitch.

EXP. 4.—Burn a minute jet of O [driven by reservoir (1) from holder (3) as in **frontispiece**] in a jar of H, quickly igniting the jet by passing through burning H at the mouth. (See NOTE EXP. 26.) [Bore hole in receiver (1) with rat-tail file moistened frequently by turpentine.]

EXP. 5.—Connect H and O holders with oxy-hydrogen blowpipe (Fig. 17), and igniting the H first, turn on the O. Place small piece of fine Pt wire (fused into glass holder, Fig. 40) in the flame. It melts. [The rubber cork in the H holder should be well oiled and firmly bound down by strong twine fastened to shoulder of the bottle. The H should be drawn into a test-tube over water and tested *before* it is burned in the blowpipe. If it burns quietly after taking fire it is safe to ignite jet. If it burns explosively, it is mixed with air and must not be ignited. The holder is first filled *completely* with water and the H (from generator as FRONTISPIECE 2) or O pressing backward expels the water, the reservoir being kept so that the water in it shall be only about a decimeter above the water in the holder. Common illuminating gas may be used instead of hydrogen with practically the same results.]

Exp. 6.—Into a tube closed at one end (through which Pt wires are fused with the internal ends almost but not quite touching) filled and inverted over mercury, put 2 cu. cm. of O and 4 cu. cm. of H and explode by electric current. The mercury rises and with the water above completely fills the tube (except perhaps a bubble of gas, which is the result of inaccurate measurement). Composition of water is proved by *synthesis*, as nothing is found dissolved in the water.

CHLORINE.

Exp. 7.—Mix in the dark, dry Cl and dry H in a stout bottle, and with care explode *by sudden exposing to direct sunshine*. H Cl fumes are formed.

Exp. 8.—Fill jar with H Cl gas and make hydrochloric acid fountain similar to ammonia fountain of Fig. 22.

SULPHUR.

Exp. 9.—Repeat Exp. 92 and afterward immerse rose in dilute sulphuric acid. The color is restored to nearly the original tint.

Exp. 10.—Place in a small flask (*provided with safety tube* as in Fig. 25, or as in H_2S generator in FRONTISPIECE 2) pieces of copper wire (or "drop copper") and add as much strong H_2SO_4 as will not quite cover the copper. Carefully heat until gas begins to be evolved and then regulate heat; else the liquid froths from too violent reaction.

$$Cu + 2H_2SO_4 = CuSO_4 + 2H_2O + SO_2$$

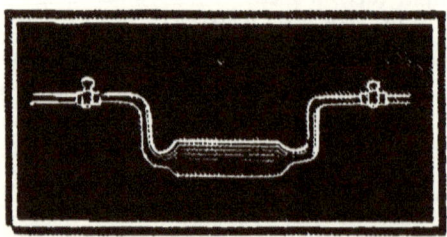

Fig. 45—SO_2 Condenser.

Pass through small condenser and connect condenser with apparatus (SO_2 condenser) shown in Fig. 45, which is immersed in a freezing mixture (ice and salt). SO_2 is easily condensed by "*cold*" to a liquid. Turn stop-cocks and preserve. Wire stop-cocks (Fig. 46) on rubber connectors (boiled in paraffine) may be used in place of glass stop-cocks.

S O_2 may also be condensed in *strong* glass tube (drawn to a point at one end) by pressure of a plunger with close-fitting, greased rubber head. When pressure (at 15°) reaches one and one-half atmospheres, drops appear on the side, and liquid S O_2 gathers in the lower part of the tube. If plunger is quickly withdrawn a part is frozen (by cold produced by *sudden evaporation*) into a snow-white solid.

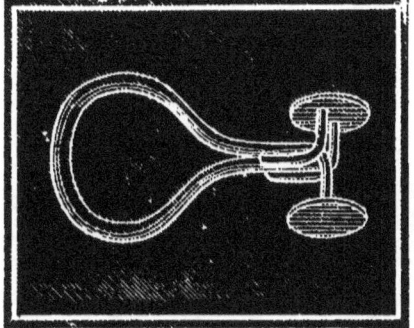

Fig. 46--Spring Stop-Cock.

Place water in a small platinum or other thin-walled dish and pour around it a little liquid S O_2. Blow with bellows to hasten evaporation of S O_2. The rapid vaporization produces a cold (—50°) so great (absorbs so much heat) that the water is quickly frozen. Mercury may be frozen if used instead of water. (It must not be put in platinum dish—why?) If S O_2 be evaporated in the receiver of an air-pump, a part will be solidified (frozen) forming snow-like solid.

PHOSPHORUS.

EXP. 11.—In a flask place a few minute pieces of P and cover with strong solution of caustic potash. Displace the air in the flask by passing H through the stopple of flask until the bubbles caught over pneumatic tube of water burn quietly. Close by wire spring (Fig. 46) the rubber tube through which H is admitted and heat flask.

$$3 \, K \, H \, O \; + \; P_4 \; + \; 3 \, H_2 O \; = \; 3 \, K \, H_2 \, P \, O_2 \; + \; H_3 P$$

The hydrogen phosphide (phosphine) takes fire because vapor of liquid $P_2 H_4$ is present and the beautiful white rings of smoke ascend. (Pure $H_3 P$ is not spontaneously inflammable.) Remove heat and pass H as before and throw away poisonous liquid.

Caution.—Perform in a well ventilated room and immediately open doors and windows after the experiment.

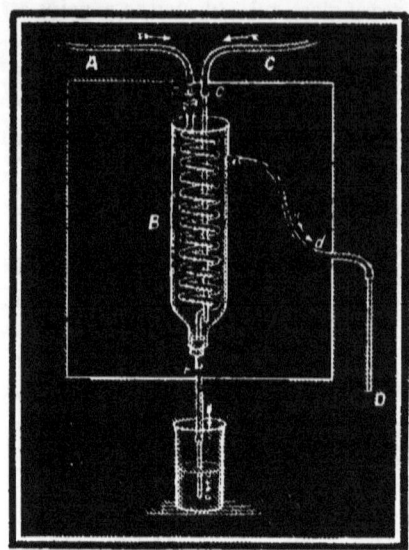

Fig. 47. A—from flask. B—condenser. C D— cold water. a b c d—rubber tubes to exclude light.

EXP. 12.—The **best test** for the element **phosphorus** (paste, rat poison) is that of distillation. Place suspected substance in flask, add dilute sulphuric acid and pass vapor through a glass condenser (set in a perfectly *dark* box painted with black pigment on the inside) and into water (Fig. 47). Look into the box by means of a small tube, while the head, like the photographer's in adjusting his camera, is covered by dark cloth or shawl. The vapor is distinctly *phosphorescent* if even a minute quantity of *free* P is present in substance. The test determines with absolute certainty whether free phosphorus is present. In cases of poisoning this test must be applied without long exposure to the air, as P in presence of *organic matter* and *air* rapidly oxidizes.

ARSENICUM AND ANTIMONY.

EXP. 13.—Place a small piece of clean copper wire in arsenical solution acidulated with hydrochloric acid, and boil. (H N O_3 must not be present.) Arsenicum is deposited on the copper. Wash, carefully dry and heat *slowly* in closed glass tube; octahedral crystals of As_2O_3 are deposited. (**Reinsch's test.**)

EXP. 14.—Generate hydrogen by heating to near the boiling point a strong solution of Na H O and Zn.

$$Zn + 2 Na H O = Na_2 Zn O_2 + H_2$$

Add a few drops of a solution of "arsenic," and pass gas through wash-bottle of lead acetate solution to remove accidental traces of H_2S; spread over mouth of wash-bottle filter paper moistened with Ag N O_3.

$$H_3 + As = H_3 As$$

$$H_3As + 3 H_2O + 6 Ag N O_3 = H_3As O_3 + 6 H N O_3 + Ag_6$$

The free silver turns the paper *purplish-black*. (**Fleitmann's test** distinguishes arsenicum *in presence of* antimony.)

GOLD.

EXP. 15.—To a solution of an auric salt (Au Cl$_3$) add H$_2$S. A brown precipitate of Au$_2$S$_3$ falls, soluble in (H$_4$N)$_2$S$_2$.

$$2 \text{ Au Cl}_3 + 3 \text{ H}_2\text{S} = \text{Au}_2\text{S}_3 + 6 \text{ H Cl}$$

EXP. 16.—To solution of salt of gold (Au Cl$_3$) add ferrous sulphate, and set aside for awhile.

$$2 \text{ Au Cl}_3 + \underset{\substack{\text{ferrous}\\\text{sulphate}}}{6 \text{ Fe S O}_4} = \underset{\substack{\text{free}\\\text{gold}}}{\text{Au}_2} + \underset{\substack{\text{ferric}\\\text{chloride}}}{\text{Fe}_2\text{Cl}_6} + \underset{\substack{\text{ferric}\\\text{sulphate}}}{2 \text{ Fe}_2 3 \text{ S O}_4}$$

Boil precipitate of free gold in H Cl, mix with equal bulk of borax and fuse in *strong* blowpipe flame. A "button" of pure gold is obtained.

EXP. 17.—Add a few drops of solution of stannous and stannic chlorides (Cl water put into Sn Cl$_2$ gives Sn Cl$_4$) to dilute solution of Au Cl$_3$, a purplish, finely-divided precipitate, "purple of Cassius" (composition doubtful), falls. The same precipitate is slowly obtained, if tin foil is placed in solution of Au Cl$_3$.

SILVER.

EXP. 18.—Sink a small piece of unsized paper into Na Cl solution for five minutes. Dry. In a *dark* box dip it beneath Ag N O$_3$ solution for one minute. Lay this "prepared paper" upon a flattened leaf which lies upon glass. Cover with an old book cover and expose the glass to sunlight. A white "picture" of the leaf is formed. Remove paper, and in dark box "fix" by dipping into sodium hyposulphite (Na$_2$ S O$_2$ or *hot* Na Cl solution) for five minutes. Wash by dipping alternately for three minutes at a time into sodium hyposulphite and then into clear water. If glass is used in place of paper to hold the Ag N O$_3$ and Na Cl, a "negative" of the leaf is formed.

MERCURY.

EXP. 19.—In a solution of salt of Hg place a clean (by H N O$_3$ and afterward H$_2$O) copper wire. It is soon coated with a mirror of Hg, more apparent if dried by blotting-paper and gently burnished with soft cloth. An equivalent amount of copper passes into the solution to take the place of the displaced Hg. Cut off the mirrored end of the wire, and, placing in closed glass tube, heat. Hg distills and globules of the metal gather upon the sides of the tube.

In almost any solution containing soluble compound of Hg, it may be detected by this *test*. No test for Hg should be considered complete unless metallic globules are obtained. A lens will often reveal the globules, if the amount of mercury is exceedingly small.

EXP. 20.—To mercuro*us* nitrate add K I, *green* mercuro*us* iodide (Hg_2I_2) falls. To mercur*ic* nitrate add K I, *red* mercur*ic* iodide ($Hg I_2$) falls (EXP. 10). Wash, dry, place in cold tube, and sublime. $Hg I_2$ condenses on the sides of the tube in *yellow* crystals; rub crystals with stick, they change to the original *red*. This change of color may be repeated indefinitely.

COPPER.

EXP. 21.—Into a solution of a copper salt (as $Cu\ S\ O_4$) put a piece of clean iron. It is coated with copper, an equivalent amount of iron passing into solution.

$$Cu\ S\ O_4\ +\ Fe\ =\ Fe\ S\ O_4\ +\ Cu \text{ (deposited on iron).}$$

EXP. 22.—Add $H_4\ N\ H\ O$ to cupric solution, a characteristic *blue* precipitate soluble in excess of $H_4N\ H\ O$ is obtained.

$$Cu\ 2\ N\ O_3\ +\ 2\ H_4\ N\ H\ O\ =\ 2\ H_4\ N\ N\ O_3\ +\ \underset{\text{precipitate}}{Cu\ 2\ H\ O}$$

ALUMINIUM.

EXP. 23.—Thoroughly char on platinum foil, bread containing **alum.** Pulverize and boil in dilute H Cl, filter, neutralize with ammonium hydrate; a fine precipitate of $Al_2\ 6\ H\ O$ (having *very distinct surface* as it settles) falls. Set aside; minute, distinct crystals appear.

CALCIUM.

EXP. 24.—Heat in oxy-hydrogen blowpipe flame the sharpened end of a stick of quicklime, a dazzling light is emitted ("lime light"). (Do not look steadily at the light.)

APPENDIX. 155

BARIUM AND STRONTIUM.

Fig. 47.—Green Fire.

EXP. 25.—Pulverize separately with great care Ba 2 N O_3 (oxidizing and coloring agent), K Cl O_3 (oxidizing agent), and gum shellac (C and H principally, combustible body). Add *one d 'op* of strong H Cl to the barium chlorate powder and mix carefully and thoroughly equal bulk of each upon piece of paper. Place on wire gauze in shoal pan and ignite, using the paper as a fuse. It gives *green* fire.

EXP 26.—Repeat EXP. 25, using Sr 2 N O_3 instead of Ba 2 N O_3. *Red* fire results.

ORGANIC CHEMISTRY.

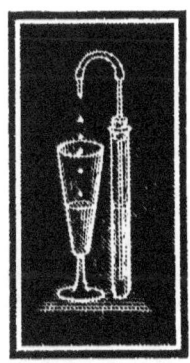

Fig. 48.

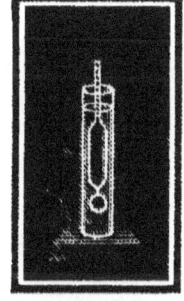

Fig. 49.

EXP. 27.—Repeat **sugar** test, EXP. 132. Albumen, if present, must be removed by boiling and filtering. Earthy phosphates should be removed by adding caustic potash to alkaline reaction and filtering. The caustic potash used must have been kept in the best Bohemian glass bottles, and not in bottles containing *lead;* otherwise Pb O falls and is mistaken for Cu_2 O. A mere yellow color is not sufficient, there must be an *actual precipitate, without prolonged boiling.* Perform the same experiment without heating, but set test-tube away for twelve hours instead. The Cu_2 O is precipitated.

EXP. 28.—Fill a test-tube entirely full of clear animal secretion containing sugar; add a small quantity of yeast and close the mouth of the test-tube by a rubber cork, through which runs a fine glass tube nearly to the bottom of the test-tube (Fig. 48). Set in a warm place for ten or twelve hours. The CO_2, produced by the fermentation, collects in the top of the test-tube, and forces the liquid out of the fine glass tube. This *Fermentation Test* is an excellent one for sugar *in animal secretions*.

Exp. 29.—Take the sp. gr. of a liquid containing sugar before fermentation and after; every "degree" lost corresponds to the presence of 21 mgs. of sugar in 10 cu. cm. of the liquid ("1 grain of sugar per fluid ounce"). That is, if urinometer (Fig. 49) shows 1050 before and 1030 after fermentation, there are 420 mgs. of sugar in 10 cu. cm. of the liquid (or 20 grains per fluid ounce). This is *Roberts' quantitative test*.

Exp. 30.—Add a small quantity of **albumen** (Exp. 138) to distilled water, or to animal secretion filtered. Upon pure, colorless, nitric acid, in test-tube of small diameter, slightly inclined, allow the liquid to trickle from a pipette. A sharp, white zone appears at the junction of the two liquids, not dissipated by heat. This is an excellent test for albumen. (Urates, if present in excess, produce a somewhat similar white zone, but the zone is dissipated by heat much less than the boiling point. Be careful not to mistake the mere mixing of the zone by boiling, for dissipation. If liquid is highly colored, of course albumen will be tinged with the color.)

Exp. 31.—Add to animal secretion containing albumen, a few drops of strong caustic potash, and filter. Add nitric acid to distinct acid reaction and boil. White coagula appear (greenish, if bile is present, brownish-red, if blood is present). A good test for albumen. (Rarely it is necessary to allow to cool, and then boil the second time.)

Exp. 32.—Precipitate a large amount of albumen from solution (Exp. 138) in distilled water, by adding nitric acid and boiling. Filter, wash, and dry over water-bath. Arrange a dozen narrow, deep test-tubes nearly filled with the acid water. Carefully weigh out, by means of a fine pair of scales (any chemist will allow the use of his scales), 5, 10, 15....55, 60 mgs. of albumen powder, and placing in each test-tube respectively, allow about three times as long for settling because of dryness of albumen. By means of a *very fine*, sharp file, carefully mark the height of the precipitated albumen. Reserve test-tubes for quantitative testing for albumen. For example: If 5 cu. cm. of liquid to be tested were placed in first test-tube, and the precipitated albumen reaches to the mark on the test-tube, 1 mg. of albumen is present in every cu. cm. of the liquid. This is a very convenient approximate *quantitative test* for albumen.

APPENDIX. 157

TESTS FOR THE ALKALOIDS.

EXP. 33.—Upon small piece of a salt of **morphia** on glass slide, place a drop of water. Warm till salt is dissolved. Place beside it a minute drop of strong *neutral* solution of perchloride of iron ($Fe_2 Cl_6$). Bring together by glass rod, a dirty-blue color results.

EXP. 34.—To solution of a salt of morphia, add sodium carbonate solution A white precipitate falls, crystalline if solution is dilute. Test as in EXP. 33 above.

EXP. 35.—Moisten a salt of morphia with nitric acid; an orange-red color results.

EXP. 36.—To a few drops of an aqueous solution of opium, add drop by drop neutral solution of perchloride of iron. A red solution of meconate of iron is formed, not destroyed by addition of corrosive sublimate solution.

EXP. 37.—Heat morphia on platinum foil, it burns and leaves no residue.

EXP. 38.—To solution of **quinine** (or of its salts) slightly acidulated with H Cl, add fresh chlorine water, and then ammonia water; a green coloration is produced.

EXP. 39.—Repeat EXP. 38, but add potassium ferrocyanide before adding ammonia; an *evanescent* red coloration appears.

EXP. 40.—Upon quinine (or its salts) let fall a few drops of strong sulphuric acid. It dissolves, producing faint yellow color.

EXP. 41.—Repeat EXP. 40, with quinine that has been adulterated with the cheaper salicin, a *deep red* color appears.

EXP. 42.—Dissolve quinine in *cold* nitric acid; a colorless solution is formed. Heat, it turns yellowish.

EXP. 43.—Heat quinine on platinum foil, no residue is left.

EXP. 44.—Place a small particle of **strychnia** on a white dish and near it a small piece of potassium bichromate. Add a drop of strong sulphuric acid to each and after a few moments bring the bichromate upon the strychnine drop with a glass rod; a vivid purple color appears, rapidly fading into yellowish red.

EXP. 45.—Upon a drop of dilute solution of strychnia on glass slide, place drop of potassium sulphocyanide; a white precipitate appears. Examine with microscope and tufts of auricular crystals are seen.

EXP. 46.—Add strong sulphuric acid to a crystal of strychnia and heat *over water-bath;* it is unaffected.

EXP. 47.—Add strong, cold nitric acid to a crystal of strychnia; it is unaffected. Heat, it turns yellow but does not dissolve.

EXP. 48.—Place a small frog in water containing traces of strychnia and in two or three hours (sooner if stronger solution is used) a slight jar throws him into the characteristic tetanic spasms.

EXP. 49.—Place a drop of tincture of **aconite** upon the skin, a tingling sensation is produced followed by prolonged numbness.

EXP. 50.—To a solution of **atropia** (belladonna) add a few drops of perchloride of gold; a yellow precipitate appears.—One drop of *very dilute* aqueous solution, applied directly to interior of eyelid, powerfully dilates the pupil.

NOTES.

(1) Uncrystallizable substances (colloids) in solution diffuse slowly through a septum, as parchment paper; while crystallizable substances (crystalloids) diffuse rapidly. If a small hoop, covered with parchment paper and filled with mixed solution, be floated upon water the crystalloids pass rapidly through while the colloids principally remain behind. This process of separation is called **Dialysis.** The so-called "dialyzed iron" is the colloid, the basic oxy-chloride of iron. (2) See larger works as to properties of CO_2, as to condensation of H; and late scientific journals as to whether shellac may not be principally an animal product. (3) The soap bubble experiment, page 51, sometimes fails because too strong acid is used, and acid moisture being carried over in the draft makes the bubble brittle. But inquiries as to "what's the matter?" is a fruitful source of chemical knowledge.

QUANTITATIVE TEST FOR CARBON DIOXIDE IN SCHOOLROOMS (AS AN INDEX TO THE AMOUNT OF POISONOUS "ANIMAL VAPOR" PRESENT).

The proportion of carbon dioxide is generally estimated by *volume* and on a scale of so many parts in 10,000 of air. In pure out-door air there are about 4 parts of carbon dioxide in 10,000 of air. In the school-room the proportion should never rise above 8 parts. Examination of the following reactions and explanations will reveal the simplicity of the test.

$$Ba\,2\,H\,O \underset{\substack{\text{barium}\\ \text{hydrate}\\ 171}}{} + H_2C_2O_4, 2\,H_2O \underset{\substack{\text{crystallized}\\ \text{oxalic acid}\\ 126}}{} = Ba\,C_2O_4 \underset{\substack{\text{barium}\\ \text{oxalat}}}{} + 4\,H_2O \underset{\text{water}}{}$$

$$Ba\,2\,H\,O \underset{171}{} + C\,O_2 \underset{44}{} = Ba\,C\,O_3 + H_2O$$

In neutralizing power.

126 gms. of cr. oxalic acid = 171 gms. of barium hydrate.
44 gms. of CO_2 = 171 " " "
therefore 44 gms. of CO_2 = 126 " of cr. oxalic acid.
1 gm. CO_2 = 2.863 + gms., or 2863 mgs. of cr. ox. acid.

If we weigh carefully 2863 mgs. of cr. oxalic acid (*not deliquesced*) and dissolve in 1,000 cu. cm. (litre) of distilled water, then 1 cu. cm. of that "standard" solution will equal (in neutralizing power) *1 milligram* of carbon dioxide. [Keep solution in dark bottle. Prepare new solution of aci every two or three weeks. The most important thing in the test is that the oxalic acid solution be fresh and made from perfect crystals.]

We then make a solution of barium hydrate dissolving about 5 gms. in a litre of water.

Suppose a jug (bottle) with tight-fitting rubber cork holds 4,155 cu. cm. (carefully measured), which jug we fill from the air of the schoolroom by means of a small bellows (blown a sufficient number of times, say 25), and take temperature of the room at the same time as 20°. Into this we pour from a sp. gr. bottle (holding with the glass stopper in, 100 cu. cm.) 100 cu. cm. of the barium hydrate solution and shake thoroughly at intervals. We now fill the burette (FRONTISPIECE 5) with the "standard" solution of oxalic acid, to a point a little above 0 and run it down carefully drop by drop to the 0 point precisely. Measuring from barium hydrate solution (by means of another sp. gr. bottle holding 50 cu. cm.) 50 cu. cm. we pour it into a clean, wide-mouthed bottle, rinse with distilled water and pour this in also. We now add a little blue litmus solution (or brown solution of turmeric). Open the burette and allow the acid to run slowly (the last drop by drop) into the wide-mouthed bottle containing the 50 cu. cm. of barium hydrate solution. It takes say 24.5 cu. cm. of acid to neutralize the alkali—when the last drop needed is added the litmus suddenly turns red (turmeric turns yellow). Now carefully fill the second sp. gr. bottle (holding 50 cu. cm.) with the solution *taken from the jug* containing the schoolroom air. Again fill the burette as before and see how many cu. cm. of the acid are required to neutralize the 50 cu. cm. taken from the jug We find in every case it requires *less*, because the carbon dioxide in the jug has already neutralized part of it. It requires, say, 22 cu. cm. of the acid. 24.5 cu. cm. − 22 cu. cm. = 2.5 cu. cm. But from equations above we know that 1 cu. cm. of the acid corresponds to 1 mg. of carbon dioxide; therefore as we poured out only one-half of the alkali to test there were 5 mgs. of carbon dioxide in the jug. From table we see that 1 mg. of carbon dioxide at 20° occupies .544470 cu. cm. of space, therefore 5 mgs. occupy 2.72235 cu. cm. The question then becomes,— If in 4055 (4155−100) cu. cm. of air there are 2.72235 cu. cm. of carbon dioxide, how much carbon dioxide in 10,000 cu. cm. of air? We have the proportion

4,055 : 10,000 :: 2.72235 :

from which we obtain 6.7 parts in 10,000 as the answer, that is, the room is fairly ventilated.

Space occupied by 1 mg. of CO_2 at different temperatures (barom. 760 mm.).

Degree C	Degree F	Cubic Cm.	Degree C	Degree F	Cubic Cm.	Degree C	Degree F	Cubic Cm.
0	32	.507306	21	69.8	.546328	28	82.4	.559336
15	59	.535178	22	71.6	.548186	29	84.2	.561104
16	60.8	.537037	23	73.4	.550044	30	86.	.563052
17	62.6	.538895	24	75.2	.551903	31	87.8	.564910
18	64.4	.540753	25	77.	.553761	32	89.6	.566769
19	66.2	.542611	26	78.8	.555610	33	91.4	.568627
20	68	.544470	27	80.6	.557477	34	93.2	.570495
						35	95.	.572343

A factor can be worked out for each jug used and for each temperature, so that by a simple multiplication of the difference shown by the burette the result is obtained. [The factor of this jug for this temperature is 2.68+. Dif. by burette 2.5 × 2.68+ = 6.7+.] Any bright pupil can master the test in a few hours and can apply it in a few minutes by using factors. The test can be made after school or before school the next day. Such tests regularly reported would do much to awaken an interest in having a proper system of ventilation.

SECTION E.

METRIC SYSTEM.

LINEAR.

10 Millimetres (mm.)	= 1 Centimetre (cm.)	
10 Centimetres	= 1 Decimetre (dcm.)	
10 Decimetres	= 1 **Metre** (m)	
10 Metres	= 1 Dekametre	
10 Dekametres	= 1 Hektometre	
10 Hektometres	= 1 Kilometre	

CAPACITY.

10 Millilitres	= 1 Centilitre
10 Centilitres	= 1 Decilitre
10 Decilitres	= **1 Litre**
10 Litres	= 1 Dekalitre
10 Dekalitres	= 1 Hektolitre
10 Hektolitres	= 1 Kilolitre

WEIGHTS.

10 Milligrams (mg.)	= 1 Centigram (cgm.)
10 Centigrams	= 1 Decigram (dcg.)
10 Decigrams	= **1 Gram** (gm.)
10 Grams	= 1 Dekagram
10 Dekagrams	= 1 Hektogram
10 Hektograms	= 1 { Kilogram (kgm.) or Kilo
1,000 Kilograms	= 1 Metric Ton (M. T.)

1 Metre (meter)	= 39.37 inches.
1 Litre	= 61 cubic inches.
1 Litre	= 1 cubic decimetre.
1 Gram	= 15.43 grains.
1 Gram	= weight of 1 cu. cm. of water 4°)
1 Kilogram	= 2 1-5 lbs.
1 Kilogram	= weight of 1 cu. dcm.(litre) of water (4°)

1 Decimetre = 10 Centimetres.

REFERENCE TABLE No. 2—CONTINUED.

NEGATIVE GROUPINGS.

Monad:
- $P\,O_4$ = metaphosphate
- $C_5 H_9 O_5$ = valerianate
- $C\,N\,O$ = cyanate
- $C\,H\,O_2$ = formate
- $C_4 H_7 O_2$ = butyrate (butter)
- $C_7 H_5 O_2$ = benzoate
- $N\,O_2$ = nitrite

Dyad:
- $C_3 H_4 O_3$ = lactate
- $C_5 H_2 N_4 O_3$ = urate
- $B_4 O_7$ = tetraborate (borax)
- $Mn\,O_4$ = manganate
- $Mn_2 O_8$ = permanganate
- $Cr_2 O_7$ = bichromate

Triad:
- $C_4 H_3 O_5$ = malate
- $C_7 H O_7$ = meconate (opium)
- $C_7 H_3 O_5$ = gallate
- $C_{27} H_{19} O_{17}$ = tannate

Tetrad:
- $Fe\,(C\,N)_6$ = ferrocyanide

Hexad:
- $Fe_2 (C\,N)_{12}$ = ferricyanide

POSITIVE GROUPING.

Monad:
- $H_2 N$ = amidogen

APPENDIX. 161

SUGGESTIONS FOR STUDENTS USING THE ANALYTICAL CHARTS.

In most schools this should be a volunteer class and the work extra, put in after school hours or on Saturdays. Be sure you want to do the work before you undertake it. Don't talk to others while at work, except in rare instances so far as quietly to obtain information. Don't "fool" in the laboratory and report those who insist upon doing it, that they may be promptly removed from the class. Have no false honor about this, for the nonsense of one may vitiate all *accurate* work for a class.—Reserve a portion of the original solution to begin upon again in case of accident, also for special tests.—Common drinking water, boiled, cooled, and filtered, usually answers for all work with the first two Groups; but distilled water must be used for the other Groups, and is better for all reagents.—Precipitate *thoroughly* each Group, but on the other hand avoid much *excess* of the precipitating reagent.—Evaporate filtrates if they become too dilute. A coal-oil stove makes a cheap source of heat for evaporation.—Avoid breathing, to any great extent, fumes of hot HCl, H_4NHO, HNO_3, aqua regia, etc. Hold dishes at arms' length while pouring such liquids. Under a gas chimney with flame at base to increase draft, is the proper place to generate noxious fumes; but such work may be easily done upon a shelf by open window with slight outward draft.—Make $(H_4N)_2S$ by passing H_2S into dilute H_4NHO (10%) till saturated and then add equal volume of H_4NHO. Digest this with a little S and filter to make $(H_4N)_2S_2$ (*yellow*), or expose $(H_4N)_2S$ to air for sufficient time.—A convenient H_2S generator is shown in FRONTISPIECE (2). The middle bulb contains Fe S. A test-tube with small hole in bottom (containing a little broken glass upon which is Fe S), lowered into wide-mouthed bottle of dilute H_2SO_4 and test-tube closed by perforated rubber stopple through which is glass tube connected with rubber tube held by spring, Fig. 46, makes a cheap H_2S apparatus.—Fig. 50 shows a convenient reagent bottle with pipetted stopple. Take test-tube to bottle to add reagent, not bottle to test-tube, and be careful not to stir up any sediment which may have fallen in case drinking water has been used.—Fig. 51 represents a system of *rapid filtration*. The stream of water must be regulated. The longer the tube *a*, the more rapid the filtering. Chamber *b* must be air-tight at top. Pt (foil) funnel-shaped tip must support filter paper at bottom, and the wet edges of filter paper must be pressed firmly against upper part of funnel. A p:rtial vacuum is formed in chamber *b* and flask *c*.—For color of precipitates, additional tests, etc., see EXP. 97 and INDEX, also have a work on *Qualitative Analysis* upon the desk for reference.

CHEMICAL PRIMER.

I. Add H Cl (15 per cent.) drop by drop till upon settling no precipitate falls. .... Filter.

Precipitate....Hg_2Cl_2, Ag Cl, Pb Cl_2, insoluble chlorides. Wash twice with cold water (Fig. 7), drain, and washing from paper with wash-bottle into beaker, boil for one minute, and........................Filter while hot.	Filtrate .. soluble chlorides of other metals, Cu, Bi, Fe, Mg....also traces of Pb Cl_2.
Precipitate.....Hg_2Cl_2, Ag Cl. Wash with hot water to remove all of the Pb Cl_2, if Pb has been found, drain, and add *warm* H_4N H O (15%), pouring it through two or three times. The ammonia water dissolves Ag Cl but reacts with Hg_2Cl_2.	Filtrate......Pb Cl_2 (Hot water dissolves Pb Cl_2) (1) Place drop of filtrate on glass and slowly evaporate white needle-shaped crystals of Pb Cl_2 are left, touch with drop of K I solution, yellow Pb I_2 appears. Divide filtrate into three portions and to first portion (2) Add $H_2S O_4$ (15%), *white* Pb S O_4 falls. To second portion (3) Add $K_2Cr_2O_7$ (3%) *yellow* Pb Cr O_4 falls. To third and *largest* portion (4) Add $(H_4N)_2$S, *black* Pb S falls. Fuse with little K_2CO_3 on charcoal in reducing (near) flame of the blowpipe. Lead globule is obtained with yellow incrustation on charcoal. Globule is malleable. (Bi and Sb are brittle.)

| Precipitate H_2N Hg_2 Cl = amido-mercurous chloride *black*. (If no black color appears no mercury in *ous* form is present.) Dissolve in beaker a portion in five or six drops of aqua regia and evaporate *carefully* nearly to dryness, dilute and test solution of Hg Cl_2 (1) by EXP. 19, APPENDIX, or (2) by adding a drop of Sn Cl_2 and white Hg_2Cl_2 is precipitated. Add excess of Sn Cl_2 and gray metallic Hg falls forming into globule if boiled with H Cl. | Filtrate...Ag Cl Add H N O_3(15%) to acid reaction. Ag Cl is reprecipitated because its solvent is neutralized. Filter, ...wash....and fuse on charcoal as in EXP. 113, obtaining silver globule with no incrustation on coal. | |

II. Evaporate filtrate from first group to small bulk, add ten drops of strong H Cl and evaporate carefully nearly to dryness. Dilute with hot H_2O and pass H_2S gas through hot solution .... Filter.

Precipitate......insoluble sulphides of Hg (ic), Cu, Pb, Bi, Sn, Sb, As (Au, Pt). Wash with hot water........*digest* ten minutes in $(H_4N)_2S_2$ (*yellow*)...........................Filter	Filtrate ≠olub:e chlorides of other metals Co, Fe, Mn, Mg, etc.
Precipitate...Hg, Cu, Pb, Bi (sulphides). Wash with hot water, add strong, boiling hot H·N O_3, pouring it on several times. ....Filter.............	Filtrate...Sn, Sb, As (Au, Pt) sulph.ides. Add dilute H Cl, sulphides are reprecipitated ...filter, drain well, boil in little strong H Cl........ ....Filter.

Ppt....,Hg. Dissolve in aqua regia and test as in First Group.	Filtrate ....Cu, Pb, Bi. Add five drops strong $H_2S O_4$ and boil down to small bulk. Pb gives white precipitate. ....Filter............	Precipitate...As, yellow. Wash and confi.m by digesting in $(H_4N)_2$ C O_3 and reprecipitating in filtrate As_2O_3 by H Cl, otherwise S from decomposition of $(H_4N)_2S_2$ may be mistaken for As.	Filtrate..Sn,Sb. Dilute with water and place a small piece of clean Zn, and of clean Pt wire in the solution. Sb forms a *distinct* black stain upon Pt.
Precipitate Pb Add H_4N HO...	Filtrate.......Bi, Cu. ....Filter.		
Ppt..Bi white. Fuse with K_2 C O_3 on charcoal... brittle globule.	F.ltrate..Cu, *deep blue* s↑lution...test by EXP. 21, APP.	Wash Pt wire. Dissolve in hot dilute H N O_3, remove wire, evaporate to dryness, add few drops dilute H Cl and pass H_2S. *Orange-yellow* precipitate, turns grayish-black by EXP. 110.—After Zn has all dissolved, filter and add drop of Hg Cl_2, white precipitate of Hg_2Cl_2 indicates Sn.—(Au and Pt rarely occur in solution)	

ANALYTICAL CHARTS. 163

III. To filtrate from second group add H_4N H O till alkaline (avoid excess), then add H_4 N Cl and $(H_4N)_2S$ and warm gently for five minutes..Filter.

Precipitate..sulphides of Ni, Co, Fe, Mn, Zn, hydrates of Cr and Al. Wash with very dilute $(H_4N)_2S$ and then with water. Add dilute H Cl breaking bottom of paper and washing through into beaker....Filter.	Filtrate... soluble compounds of metals of IV and V Group.

| Precipitate ....Ni, Co (sulphides). Fuse a portion in borax head—*blue* indicates Co. V i o l e t when hot and brown when cold indicates Ni alone. If both are present Co overpowers Ni colors.—Dissolve the remaining ppt. in few drops of aqua regia, evaporate to dryness, dissolve in few drops of water, add a little Co Cl_2 and evaporate on white paper. *Green* indicates Ni. | Filtrate....Fe, Mn, Cr, Zn, Al. evaporate carefully nearly to dryness, dilute slightly, add K H O till strongly alkaline, boil carefully 3 minutes. Filter. Ppt....Fe, Mn, Cr. Wash with hot water. Fuse a portion on Pt foil with small quantity of K_2CO_3 and KNO_3. **Deep green** indicates Mn.—Dissolve a second portion in dilute H Cl and add $K_4Fe(CN)_6$ Prussian *blue* indicates iron.— Dissolve residue in hot acetic acid and add $Pb2C_2H_3O_2$ Chrome *yellow* ppt. indicates Cr. | Add few drops of H N O_3 evaporate carefully nearly to dryness, dilute slightly, add Filtrate....Al, Zn. Add Ppt.....Zn slate-white.. Heat upon charcoal, add drop of Co Cl_2 and heat again...*green* coloration. Filtrate..Al. Add H Cl to acid reaction, boil, filter, and add dilute H4N H O to alkaline reaction a fine (flocculent if large amt. is present) precipitate shows Al. Confirm as with Zn...*blue* mass. |

IV. Evaporate filtrate from Third Group to dryness, dissolve, add few drops of H Cl, boil, filter, and to filtrate add H_4N Cl, H_4N H O to alkaline reaction, and then $(H_4N)_2CO_3$.

Precipitate ...Ba, Sr, Ca. (20%) acetic acid, add $K_2Cr_2O_7$........	Dissolve carbonates in dilute .... Filter.	Filtrate.. soluble carbonates of Fifth Group.

| Ppt.... Ba Cr O_4. *yellow*. with H Cl and apply flame test Exp. 125. | Filtrate... Sr, Ca. Add $(H_4N)_2CO_3$, filter. Dissolve precipitate in H Cl, add dilute H_2SO_4 and set aside for an hour Filter. Ppt. Sr S O_4 moisten with H Cl and apply flame test Exp. 126. | Filtrate.....Ca. Add H N H O to alkaline reaction and $(H_4N)_2C_2O_4$. Moisten white ppt. with H Cl and apply flame test. *Dull red* indicates Ca. |

V. To filtrate from Fourth Group concentrated by evaporation add H_4N H O to alkaline reaction and then **H Na_2 P O_4** let stand for ten minutes (till *cold*).

Precipitate.. *crystalline.* H_4N Mg P O_4 white shows Mg	Filtrate..... Na, K (and H_4N). Concentrate by boiling. Apply flame test. *Yellow* indicates Na, *purplish* K. If both are present the yellow obscures entirely the purplish color. Look through blue glass at flame, the Na color is not seen and the K color appears reddish-violet. Either metal may thus be detected in the presence of the other.

Tests for H_4N compounds of course must be applied to the *original* solution. Heat a portion of this with Na H O. H_3N is recognized by (1) odor, (2) turns *moist* litmus paper, suspended in mouth of (but not touching) test-tube, *blue*, and (3) by fumes with glass rod dipped in *dilute* H Cl.

Pt wire for flame tests must be *clean*, indeed, all utensils should be.— To digest is to warm *without scalding*. C. P. stands for chemically pure, and C. P. acids, etc., must be used in analytical work.—Groups IV and V are best tested with the spectroscope (which see).—$Na_2 C O_3$ may be used for $K_2C O_3$.

www.ingramcontent.com/pod-product-compliance
Lightning Source LLC
Chambersburg PA
CBHW030255170426

43202CB00009B/748